Pass your

Numeracy Skills Test

D1638431

Sam Kirkwood

Lewis Wilding

Oliver Naylor

TABLE OF CONTENTS

QTS MATHS TUTOR
WWW.QTSMATHSTUTOR.CO.UK

 Based on hundreds of reviews on Trustpilot

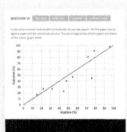
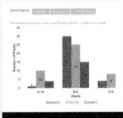

QTS LITERACY TUTOR
WWW.LITERACYSKILLSTEST.CO.UK

FREE ONLINE LITERACY SKILLS TEST
EXPERT 1 TO 1 TUITION WITH OUR QTS SPECIALISTS

—— WHAT QTS LITERACY TUTOR HAS TO OFFER ——

Spelling Practice

Punctuation Questions

Grammar Section

Comprehension Resources

Practice Tests

Expert Tutors

Correct Format

New Question Formats

Visit www.literacyskillstest.co.uk to take a Free Full Practice Test today.

10
LITERACY SKILLS TESTS

97%
LEARNER PASS RATE

490
TEST QUESTIONS

About the author

The QTS Maths Tutor book has been produced through a collaboration of QTS industry experts. A team of numeracy skills tutors and mathematicians have devised a comprehensive numeracy skills book that covers all aspects of the test, including the most up to date question types.

As part of the book, there are also links to other resources such as **videos** and **practice tests** that are regularly updated, making sure that the book remains more relevant than any others out there. The tutors and maths experts who have collaborated on the book have first-hand experience of what people struggle with when preparing for their test. This book has been designed from the student's perspective making the hints, tips and learning resources even more effective.

The QTS Maths Tutor team provides the leading numeracy skills test and tuition service in the country and this experience is clearly reflected in the contents of this book.

Visit **https://www.QTSMathsTutor.co.uk/** to access more numeracy skills resources and practice tests.

Premium Code:

PREMIUM10

Details of the QTS Skills Tests

The numeracy skills test comprises of two sections, a mental arithmetic section followed by a written data section. The 12 mental arithmetic questions require you to calculate your answers within 18 seconds of the second repeat of the question. You have to answer all 12 questions in a row and there is no option to go back. You are not permitted to use a calculator in this part of the test.

The written section is made up of 16 onscreen graph and data questions. You have a total of 36 minutes to answer questions 13 to 28 which are based on graphs, tables and data interpretation. You are permitted to use an onscreen calculator in this part of the test.

Both sections of the test require you to submit your answer onscreen, very similar to the QTS Maths Tutor interactive tests and the government practice tests which you can find online using the website links below. Many people ask, what is the pass mark for the numeracy skills test? The answer is it changes depending on the difficulty of the test. The average pass mark appears to be around 18, or 63%. Whilst doing the practice numeracy skills tests we advise that you aim to achieve 20 or more to be confident in passing the real exam.

There is more information about the skills tests, common mistakes, testing centres and much more at: **www.QTSMathsTutor.co.uk** and **http://sta.education.gov.uk/**.

QTS Maths Tutor Help Sheet

The following conversions, formulae and tips are a really good starting point to help you with the most common types of maths questions that appear in the numeracy skills test.

Fractions	Percentages	Decimals
$\dfrac{1}{2}$	50%	0.5
$\dfrac{1}{3}$	33.$\dot{3}$%	0.$\dot{3}$
$\dfrac{2}{3}$	66.$\dot{6}$%	0.$\dot{6}$
$\dfrac{1}{4}$	25%	0.25
$\dfrac{3}{4}$	75%	0.75
$\dfrac{1}{5}$	20%	0.2
$\dfrac{1}{8}$	12.5%	0.125
$\dfrac{1}{10}$	10%	0.1
$\dfrac{1}{20}$	5%	0.05

Percentage and Fractions

Calculate percentage of an amount:
$$= \left(\frac{Amount}{Original}\right) \times 100$$

Percentage Increase:
$$= \left(\frac{Increase}{Original}\right) \times 100$$

Percentage Decrease
$$= \left(\frac{Decrease}{Original}\right) \times 100$$

Fraction of an amount:	$= Fraction \times Amount$

Multiplication and Division tricks

$\times 4$	$\times 2 \ then \ \times 2 \ again$
$\div 4$	$\div 2 \ then \ \div 2 \ again$
$\times 10$	$Move \ the \ decimal \ point \ 1 \ place \ to \ the \ right$
$\div 10$	$Move \ the \ decimal \ point \ 1 \ place \ to \ the \ left$
$\div 0.1$	$\times 10$
$\times 0.1$	$\div 10$
$\div 0.2$	$\div 2 \ then \ \times 10$
$\times 0.2$	$\times 2 \ then \ \div 10$
$\div 0.25$	$\times 4$
$\times 0.25$	$\div 4$
$\div 0.5$	$\times 2$
$\times 0.5$	$\div 2$

Mean, Mode , Median and Range

Finding the mean:	$= \dfrac{Add \ up \ all \ the \ numbers}{How \ many \ numbers \ there \ are}$
Finding the range of a set:	$= Highest \ in \ a \ set - Lowest \ in \ the \ set$
Finding the median:	$Put \ the \ set \ in \ ascending \ order \ then \ find \ the \ \dfrac{n+1}{2}^{th} \ term.$
Finding the mode:	$= Most \ common \ term \ in \ set.$

Mental Arithmetic Section (Non-Calculator)

Mental arithmetic questions are often the questions that people are most fearful of. This is due to the pressure created by the **18 second time limit** which is applied to every question.

The clock starts ticking after the second repeat of the question and if you aren't confident with your mental maths, then this can be quite daunting. This section of the book comprehensively covers all of the mental arithmetic question types and topics that come up in the test.

You can use the guidance notes along with the practice and exam style questions to help you develop the methods and techniques required to successfully navigate this part of the exam.

From fractions to percentages, everything is covered and many of the skills needed are also applicable to the written data section so it is important to learn the methods and get plenty of practise using them. To practise questions in the audio format like the actual test we recommend you visit the QTS Maths Tutor website.

1. Multiplication

1.1   I can multiply numbers from 1 to 12 - SKILLS Questions

a)	9×12	j)	$5 \times 7 \times 8$	s)	$2 \times 2 \times 5$
b)	3×8	k)	$7 \times 9 \times 2$	t)	$4 \times 10 \times 5 \times 8$
c)	5×3	l)	$4 \times 11 \times 9$	u)	$11 \times 3 \times 7 \times 12$
d)	11×6	m)	$12 \times 3 \times 4$	v)	$5 \times 10 \times 7 \times 9$
e)	6×10	n)	$6 \times 11 \times 6$	w)	$9 \times 9 \times 7 \times 3$
f)	3×11	o)	$4 \times 4 \times 10$	x)	$3 \times 11 \times 4 \times 11$
g)	11×2	p)	$3 \times 11 \times 10$	y)	$2 \times 8 \times 5 \times 8$
h)	$4 \times 4 \times 11$	q)	$4 \times 12 \times 12$	z)	$2 \times 6 \times 7 \times 5$
i)	$10 \times 2 \times 12$	r)	$10 \times 10 \times 2$		

1.2   I can multiply numbers from 1 to 12 - TEST Questions

a)   Four students each run 5 kilometres on a Tuesday and 7 kilometres on every other day of the week. How many kilometres do the students run altogether in a week?

b)   At Brownhill Academy four teachers set 3 pieces of homework to each pupil in their class. If the average class size is 12, how many pieces of homework were set in total?

c)   Three teaching assistants each read 4 articles on a Thursday and 6 on a Monday. How many articles are read by the teaching assistants in one week?

d)   Three teachers each read 4 books on 7 different occasions. How many books do the teachers read altogether?

e) Three teachers purchase 2 pencils for each of the students in their class. If on average each class contains 11 pupils, how many pencils were bought in total?

f) A teacher reads over 4 sample exams for each of the pupils in his revision class separately. If there are 8 students in the class, how many sample exams does the teacher read?

g) Seven pupils each eat 2 bags of crisps, one sandwich and two chocolate bars. Altogether, how many items of food do the pupils eat?

h) At Langwith College a student reads 3 research papers on a Monday, Tuesday, Friday, Saturday and Sunday and 6 on each of the remaining days of the week. In one week, how many research papers does the student read?

i) Three pupils each eat 5 sweets on each day of the weekend. How many sweets do the pupils eat altogether?

j) Four teachers each drink two bottles of water containing 3 litres per bottle. How much water do they drink altogether? Give your answer in litres.

k) Two teaching assistants each run 3 kilometres on a Friday and 6 kilometres on 5 other days of the week. How many kilometres do they cover in total, between them, in one full week?

l) A teacher has 3 days off a month. How many days off does this equate to in 2 years?

m) Two pupils each play 4 games and repeat each game 3 times. How many times are the games played in total?

n) Two pupils require 3 maths lessons and 3 different pupils require 5 maths lessons. How many maths lessons are required in total?

o) A year group is playing games at the end of term. The first three games require 8 players. The next 8 games require 11 players. How many players do the games require in total, assuming each different player can only play one game?

p) In an art competition, two people drew 8 landscapes and 10 people drew 7 landscapes. How many landscapes did the pupils draw altogether?

q) How many puzzles will be solved if three pupils solve 12 and ten pupils each solve 2?

r) In an after school games club, the first game requires 4 players and the following 12 games require 12 players. Assuming each player is a different person, how many people play the games in total?

s) A school caretaker places storage boxes in cupboards. Two cupboards have 4 storage boxes and 5 cupboards have 7 storage boxes. How many storage boxes are there?

t) Four teachers require 11 parents to help with a festival. Another 3 teachers require 8 parents to help with the same festival. How many parents are required in total?

u) A charity buys 50 display cases each containing 1 item. Another 11 display cases are purchased each containing 4 items. How many items are there in total?

v) In one term, three weeks have 6 English lessons and 8 weeks have 4 English lessons. How many English lessons are there in total in this term?

w) Three employees require 6 breaks per week. In addition, 6 employees require 7 breaks per week. In one week, how many breaks are taken?

x) In an art room two cupboards contain 5 bottles of paint and 11 cupboards contain 2 bottles of paint. How many bottles of paint do the cupboards contain altogether?

y) Four school teams play 8 football matches. Eleven school teams play 12 football matches. How many football matches are played altogether?

z) Two Principals each need to hire 6 teachers to cover working hours in one day. If each teacher works 8 hours a day, how many hours do the Principals need to cover in total?

1.3 I can use the grid multiplication method
Introduction

There was a time when written multiplication was done in columns. This has now been replaced by the grid method of multiplication which has been part of primary school teaching since the 90s. This method requires less attention on the size of the number, i.e. how many zeros you add at the end, and this reduces the scope for error. Whether you use this method or the column method for the test you will need to know the grid method when working through your teacher training course.

Multiplication by 10, 100, 1000

To perform grid multiplication quickly it is necessary to know how to multiply 10s, 100s and 1000s together.

1. What is **100 × 200**? Well, do 1 × 2 = 2 and as there are 4 zeros in the question, stick on 4 zeros in the answer (0000). Therefore, **100 × 200 = 20000**.

2. What is **30 × 500**? Well, 3 × 5 = 15 and there are 3 zeros in the question, stick on 3 zeros in the answer (000). Therefore, 30 × 500 = 15000.

Explanation Example

Example 1

What is **12 × 3**?

1. Break up the numbers and write them out in a grid.

2. Complete the grid by multiplying the numbers together.

3. Add up the numbers and this is the answer.

$$12 \times 3$$

$$(10 + 2) \times 3$$

×	3
10	30
2	6

30 + 6 = 36

12 × 3 = 36

Example 2

What is **79 × 45**?

1. Break up the numbers and write them out in a grid.

2. Complete the grid by multiplying the numbers together.

3. Add up the numbers, writing them in columns for ease, and get your final answer.

$$79 \times 45$$

$$(70 + 9) \times (40 + 5)$$

×	40	5	Sum
70	2800	350	3150
9	360	45	405 +
			3555

79 × 45 = 3555

Example 3: Test Question

A teacher needs **71** pieces of paper per pupil. There are **40** pupils. How many pieces are needed in total?

$$71 \times 40$$

×	70	1	Sum
40	2800	40	2840

$71 \times 40 = 2840$

Example 4: Test Question

A teaching assistant buys **18** centimetres of string for every pupil. The class has **75** pupils. How many centimetres of string did she buy in total?

$$18 \times 75$$

×	70	5	Sum
10	700	50	750
8	560	40	600
			1350

$18 \times 75 = 1350$ cm

Example 5: Test Question

A teacher needs **79** millilitres of milk for every student. The class has **34** students. How many millilitres of milk are needed altogether?

$$79 \times 34$$

×	70	9	Sum
30	2100	270	2370
4	280	36	316
			2686

$79 \times 34 = 2686$ mm

1.4   I can use the grid multiplication method - SKILLS Questions

a) 42 × 4

b) 80 × 48

c) 80 × 71

d) 26 × 44

e) 45 × 15

f) 785 × 6

g) 764 × 75

h) 217 × 122

i) 799 × 572

j) 896 × 777

k) 6481 × 7

l) 8106 × 51

m) 5401 × 243

n) 5550 × 2902

o) 7638 × 5562

p) 97606 × 5

q) 84714 × 71

r) 74718 × 972

s) 69327 × 5187

t) 95236 × 59361

u) 952221 × 5

v) 360185 × 31

w) 353588 × 683

x) 456639 × 2321

y) 763424 × 84658

z) 123456 × 654321

1.5   I can use the grid multiplication method - TEST Questions

a) Two teachers each order 38 leaflets, each leaflet costs 38 pence. How much did they spend in total? Give your answer in pounds.

b) Two teachers in a school each buy 23 rulers, each ruler costs 24 pence. How much did they spend in total? Give your answer in pounds.

c) A school requires 61 exercise books per pupil during their school life. If a class has 60 pupils, how many exercise books are required altogether?

d) Two Principals in the West Midlands each order 14 posters. Another four Principals order 26 posters. How many posters did the Principals order in total?

e) A pupil in a drama group travels 28 miles to another school, each mile costs 15 pence in fuel. How much did the pupil spend on fuel? Give your answer in pounds.

f) 28 teachers in a school each buy 17 books. 3 teachers buy 18 books. How many books did the teachers buy in total?

g) Three parents each order 37 Christmas cards. A further 2 parents order 16 Christmas cards. How many Christmas cards did the parents order in total?

h) Two departments each buy 25 books. A further 3 departments buy 25 books. How many books did the different departments buy?

i) Two students each spend £15.75 on their history revision guides. How much do the students spend in total purchasing their history revision guides? Give your answer in pounds.

j) On average students use 29 pieces of stationery during a school year. If a class has 35 students, how many pieces of stationery are used in total during one school year?

k) A teaching assistant needs 95 copies of a book for the new term. Each book costs £35. What is the total cost?

l) All 31 teachers in a school each travel 26 kilometres to an event, each kilometre costs 24 pence. How much did they spend in total? Give your answer in pounds.

m) Three charities in Greater London each order 16 leaflets. Another 2 charities order 37 leaflets. How many leaflets did the charities order in total?

n) An English faculty purchases 50 copies of a teaching syllabus guide. If each copy costs £50, how much is spent in total?

o) All 20 teachers in an academy chain each bake 15 cakes for charity; on average each cake cost 33 pence to make. How much did they spend in total? Give your answer in pounds.

p) 18 children in a class each take 23 items of clothing on a school trip. Due to baggage fees, each piece of clothing costs 26 pence on average. How much did the 18 children spend on baggage fees? Give your answer in pounds.

q) 25 pupils in a class each order 24 Christmas cards. Another 2 pupils order 14 Christmas cards. How many Christmas cards did the pupils order in total?

r) Two Principals in an academy chain each organised 38 events across two years. In addition, 6 Principals organised 33 events. How many events did the Principals organise in total?

s) Two teachers each travel 13 kilometres to an event. 4 teachers each travel 27 kilometres. How many kilometres did the teachers travel altogether?

t) Two head teachers in Surrey each travel 15 miles to another school, each mile costs 14 pence. How much did they spend in total? Give your answer in pounds.

u) A school buys 31 millilitres of acid for a school experiment. The school has 95 pupils. How many millilitres of acid are purchased altogether?

v) A teaching assistant needs 40 pieces of paper for every pupil. The class has 20 pupils. How many pieces of paper are required?

w) A school fundraiser raised £25 per student. If the school had 400 students, how much was raised in total?

x) Over the period of a week a teacher spends 73 minutes marking work for every pupil in her class. If her class has 15 pupils, how long does she spend marking each week? Give your answer in minutes.

y) A head of Year requires 77 minutes to review each student's progress. The year group contains 70 students. How long does the head of year spend reviewing student progress? Give your answer in minutes.

z) What is seventy-nine multiplied by thirty-five?

1.6   I can multiply by fractions

Introduction

The multiplication of fractions is one of the easier techniques to master as it involves multiplying the tops of the fractions (numerators) together and the bottoms (denominators) together. After this, sometimes it is possible to reduce the fraction to its simplest (or lowest) form.

You will need to know how to multiply numbers together, how to reduce fractions to their simplest form and be aware that whole numbers can be written as fractions with 1 on the bottom. For example 2 is the same as $\frac{2}{1}$.

You should note that the word '**of**' in mathematics means multiply. For example, 10 lots **of** 2 bananas = **10** × **2** = **20** bananas.

Explanation Example

Example 1

What is $\frac{1}{2} \times \frac{1}{2}$?

1. Multiply the tops.
2. Multiply the bottoms.
3. Simplify if needed

$$\frac{1}{2} \times \frac{1}{2} = \frac{1}{4}$$

Example 2

What is $\frac{2}{3} \times \frac{1}{5}$?

   1.   Multiply the tops.

   2.   Multiply the bottoms.

   3.   Simplify if needed.

$$\frac{2}{3} \times \frac{1}{5} = \frac{2}{15}$$

In this instance we cannot simplify it.

Example 3

What is $\frac{2}{4} \times \frac{2}{8}$?

   1.   Multiply the tops.

   2.   Multiply the bottoms.

   3.   Simplify.

$$\frac{2}{4} \times \frac{2}{8} = \frac{1}{8}$$

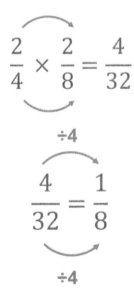

$$\frac{2}{4} \times \frac{2}{8} = \frac{4}{32}$$

$$\div 4$$

$$\frac{4}{32} = \frac{1}{8}$$

$$\div 4$$

Example 4: Test Question

In a group of **250** students, $\frac{1}{5}$ passed the English exam. How many passed the English exam?

$$\frac{1}{5} \times \frac{250}{1} = \frac{250}{5}$$

÷5

$$\frac{250}{5} = \frac{50}{1} = 50$$

÷5

$$\frac{1}{5} of\ 250 = 50$$

Example 5: Test Question

In a year group of **96** children, $\frac{3}{4}$ of them took part in a sports day. How many of the year group did **not** take part in the sports day?

(Remember if ¾ take part, ¼ don't take part)

$$\frac{1}{4} \times \frac{96}{1} = \frac{96}{4}$$

÷4

$$\frac{96}{4} = \frac{24}{1} = 24$$

÷4

$$\frac{1}{4} of\ 96 = 24$$

1.7   I can multiply by fractions – SKILLS Questions

a) $\frac{1}{2} \times \frac{1}{3}$

g) $\frac{7}{9} \times \frac{1}{3}$

l) $\frac{1}{4} \times 100$

q) $\frac{2}{6} \times 66$

v) $\frac{4}{5} of\ 125$

b) $\frac{1}{6} \times \frac{1}{4}$

h) $\frac{8}{9} \times \frac{2}{5}$

m) $\frac{1}{3} \times 99$

r) $\frac{3}{8} \times 40$

w) $\frac{6}{8} of\ 88$

c) $\frac{1}{3} \times \frac{1}{6}$

i) $\frac{6}{7} \times \frac{6}{7}$

n) $\frac{1}{5} \times 125$

s) $\frac{5}{8} \times 80$

x) $\frac{2}{3} of\ 45$

d) $\frac{2}{3} \times \frac{2}{5}$

j) $\frac{1}{9} \times \frac{1}{1}$

o) $\frac{1}{8} \times 200$

t) $\frac{1}{7} \times 49$

y) $\frac{7}{9} of\ 63$

e) $\frac{1}{3} \times \frac{2}{8}$

k) $\frac{1}{2} \times 30$

p) $\frac{2}{3} \times 66$

u) $\frac{1}{2} of\ 64$

z) $\frac{6}{7} of\ 49$

f) $\frac{3}{7} \times \frac{4}{6}$

1.8   I can multiply by fractions – TEST Questions

a) The total cost of a school trip is £350 per pupil. $\frac{1}{10}$ of this cost is travel, which is covered by the school. How much will each pupil have to pay if they have to pay the remaining amount?

b) In an English exam $\frac{2}{8}$ of the marks were from a poetry test and $\frac{6}{8}$ from prose coursework. In the poetry test, $\frac{6}{7}$ of the marks were for spelling and punctuation. What fraction of the marks for the overall English exam was from spelling and punctuation?

c) In a school with 1200 students, $\frac{1}{12}$ passed the English exam. How many students passed the English exam?

d) In a rowing team $\frac{3}{6}$ of the team were boys and $\frac{3}{6}$ were girls. Of the boys, $\frac{2}{8}$ were A-Level students. What fraction of the rowing team were A-Level students?

e) In a French exam $\frac{6}{10}$ of the marks were from an oral exam and $\frac{4}{10}$ from a reading paper. In the oral exam, $\frac{2}{10}$ of the marks were from knowledge of nouns. What fraction of the total mark was from knowledge of nouns?

f) An assessment of 500 school chairs found that $\frac{10}{100}$ were damaged and would need replacing. How many chairs need replacing?

g) In a school with 250 pupils, $\frac{20}{100}$ achieved a Grade 5. What number of the school did not achieve a Grade 5?

h) In a class of 15 students, $\frac{4}{5}$ failed an exam. How many students failed?

i) In a group of 200 students, $\frac{1}{8}$ achieved a GCSE Grade 7. How many of the group achieved a GCSE Grade 7?

j) In a Literature exam $\frac{3}{6}$ of the marks were from a poetry test and $\frac{3}{6}$ from prose coursework. In the poetry test, $\frac{7}{8}$ of the marks were from grammar. What fraction of the Literature exam marks was from grammar?

k) On a school trip of 350 children, $\frac{6}{30}$ forgot to bring a coat. How many children did not bring a coat?

l) In a sports team $\frac{3}{10}$ of the pupils were boys and $\frac{7}{10}$ girls. Of the girls, $\frac{4}{7}$ of the pupils were from upper school. What fraction of all of the pupils were from upper school?

m) In a cookery exam $\frac{3}{8}$ of the marks were from a practical exercise and $\frac{5}{8}$ from a theory exam. In the practical exercise, $\frac{6}{7}$ of the marks were from a knowledge of food safety. What fraction of the total marks was not from knowledge of food safety?

n) In a cookery exam $\frac{6}{9}$ of the marks were from a practical exercise and $\frac{3}{9}$ from a theory exam. In the practical exercise, $\frac{2}{5}$ of the marks were from a knowledge of food safety. What fraction of the marks was from knowledge of food safety?

o) One tenth of a music group play the piano. There are 50 members in the group. How many people can play the piano?

p) In a year group of 270 children, $\frac{1}{6}$ prefer hockey to netball. How many children prefer hockey to netball?

q) For a driving test, marks were awarded as follows: $\frac{6}{9}$ of the marks were for a practical course and $\frac{3}{9}$ for a theory test. In the theory test, $\frac{7}{10}$ of the marks were for hazard perception. What fraction of the total mark was for hazard perception?

r) In a maths exam $\frac{3}{7}$ of the marks were for addition and $\frac{4}{7}$ for subtraction. For addition, $\frac{2}{3}$ of the marks were for a mental exercise. What fraction of the total marks was not from a mental exercise?

s) What is $\frac{7}{8} \times \frac{1}{2}$?

t) In a year group of 160 children, $\frac{2}{16}$ needed additional support. How many of the year group needed additional support?

u) Twenty-five out of forty-five children at Edge Grammar consume too much salt. What fraction of the children do not consume too much salt?

v) On a field trip $\frac{2}{10}$ of the species collected were insects and $\frac{8}{10}$ were worms. Of the worms, $\frac{8}{9}$ were earthworms. Overall, what fraction were earthworms?

w) In a school of 120 students, $\frac{2}{6}$ achieved a Grade 7. How many of the students achieved a Grade 7?

x) Out of a group of 70 children, $\frac{16}{32}$ passed the English exam. How many children did not pass the English exam?

y) Of 180 children, $\frac{2}{12}$ received free school meals. How many children is this?

z) In a tub of 270 sweets, $\frac{1}{6}$ were strawberry flavoured. How many sweets were not strawberry-flavoured?

1.9　I can multiply by decimals

Introduction

The method we will use to multiply decimals is explained using examples. It will require knowledge of the grid method of multiplication, which is described in section 1.3 on page 15. These can be very tricky under the time pressure of the real exam so make sure you get lots of practice.

Explanation Example

Example 1

What is **0.5 × 1.1**?

1. Ignore the decimals and convert the numbers into whole numbers.

2. Perform grid multiplication.

3. Go back to the original question and count up the amount of numbers after every decimal point.

4. You need the same number of figures after the decimal in your answer from part **2** (count from the right).

5 ×11

×	10	1	
5	50	5	55

What is 0.5 × 1.1?

55

Move 2 decimal places

0.5 × 1.1 = 0.55

Example 2: Test Question

A head teacher needs **4.3** litres of milk for each pupil. There are **3** pupils. How many litres are needed in total?

$$4.3 \times 3$$

$$43 \times 3$$

×	40	3	
3	120	9	129

What is 4.3 × 3?

12.9 litres of milk

Example 3: Test Question

What is **0.03** × **4.5**?

1. Ignore the decimals

2. Perform grid multiplication.

3. Go back to the original question and count up the amount of numbers after every decimal point.

4. You need the same number of figures after the decimal in your answer from part **2.** (Count from the right).

$$00.3 \times 45$$

$$3 \times 45$$

×	40	5	
3	120	15	135

What is 0.03 × 4.5?

135

Move 3 decimal places

0.03 × 4.5 = 0.135

Example 4: Test Question

A teaching assistant needs **3.25** centimetres of paper for each pupil. There are **6** pupils. How many centimetres are needed altogether?

$$3.25 \times 6$$
$$325 \times 6$$

×	300	20	5	
6	1800	120	30	1950

What is 3.25 × 6 ?
1950
19.5 cm of paper

1.10   I can multiply by decimals – SKILLS Questions

a)	1 × 0.1	j)	5.5 × 1.5	s)	0.13 × 1.72
b)	87 × 3.1	k)	6.5 × 6	t)	8.03 × 15.4
c)	64 × 1.2	l)	8.9 × 6.3	u)	4.003 × 3.4
d)	13.1 × 0.2	m)	5.4 × 5.8	v)	0.007 × 0.631
e)	0.5 × 0.5	n)	1.72 × 0.53	w)	0.11 × 0.666
f)	10 × 0.1	o)	4.61 × 7.88	x)	0.3817 × 7.76
g)	0.002 × 6.2	p)	0.22 × 0.86	y)	50.155 × 10.005
h)	0.125 × 3	q)	0.93 × 5.86	z)	3.044 × 7.48
i)	6.4 × 4.1	r)	0.94 × 4.72		

a)   A teacher buys 5 boxes for storage. Each box holds 6.6 kilograms. How many kilograms do the boxes hold altogether?

b)   A technology teacher requires an average of 2.5 items per student for a project they are undertaking. If there are 20 pupils in the class, how many items are needed for the project?

c)   On average a teacher requires 3.5 pieces of paper for each pupil in her class. There are 20 pupils in her class. How many pieces of paper does she need?

d)   A classroom requires 7 pieces of carpet to replace the damage. Using the fact that one piece measures 10.45 metres, what is the amount required in total?

e)   A teacher runs 3 circuits a week. Knowing that one complete circuit is 11.9 kilometres, what is the number of kilometres ran altogether?

f)   A science teacher needs 3.4 millilitres of vinegar for each student. The class has 4 students. How many millilitres are needed in total?

g)   A bench requires 2 pieces of identical wood. Knowing that one-piece measures 2.15 metres, what is the total amount of wood required?

h)   A child buys 8 boxes of toys. Using the fact that one box holds 2.85 kilograms, what is the weight of the boxes in total?

i)   A school badminton team buys 1.9 litres of juice per student. There are 5 students in the badminton team. How many litres of juice are purchased?

j)   A school requires 4.25 centimetres of rope for each pupil. There are 12 pupils. How many centimetres are required in total?

k)   A teacher buys an average of 2.9 pencils per pupil. There are 10 pupils. How many pencils does the teacher buy?

l)   3.05 millilitres of milk was given to 4 separate students. How many millilitres of milk were given in total?

m)   A science teacher needs 4.6 millilitres of acid for every pupil completing an experiment. The experiment involves 4 pupils. How many millilitres of acid are needed altogether?

n)   A teacher bought an average of 2.25 exercise books per pupil. There are 100 pupils. How many books did the teacher buy?

o)   A cupboard requires 7 tins of paint for full coverage. One tin holds 4.1 kilograms. What is the total weight of the paint required?

p)   A chemistry teacher buys 2.5 jars of chemicals for every pupil. The class has 10 pupils. How many jars did she buy altogether?

q)   A child drinks 2 bottles of water. Using the fact that one bottle holds 9.95 litres, what is the amount drunk?

r) A school hall requires 6 new blinds to replace the old ones. Each blind measures 6.7 metres wide, and when placed side to side they cover the entire length of the hall. What is the length of the school hall?

s) A head teacher runs 3 times a day. If one complete route is 7.35 kilometres, what is the number of kilometres ran in total?

t) There are 12 students in a class who on average have 3.25 pieces of stationery each. How many pieces of stationery does the class have in total?

u) A child runs 5 times a day. Each complete route is 5.45 kilometres. What is the number of kilometres they ran altogether?

v) A parent purchases 3 school jumpers for her children. If one jumper costs £10.50, what is the total cost of all 3 jumpers?

w) A classroom requires 8 new chairs. Each chair costs £8.15. What is the total cost of the furniture?

x) A student plays football 2 times a week. On average he scores 1.25 goals a game. How many goals would you expect him to score in 8 weeks?

y) A teacher requires 5 equal lengths of string. One piece of string measures 2.35 metres. What length of string is required in total?

z) A head teacher goes to a community meeting at a local centre 4.75 kilometres away from their school. What is the distance travelled by the head teacher by the time they return to school?

2. Division

Introduction

To succeed at division based questions you need to be confident with your multiplication ability, especially your times tables from 1 to 12. **See Page 12 for more help with this.**

Division is the opposite operation to multiplication.

Asking

What do we get if we divide 42 by 6?

Has the same solution as asking

What do we have to multiply by 6 to get 42?

In both instances the answer is 7.

A standard method of performing written division is the 'bus stop' method which is shown in the following examples.

Explanation Example

Example 1

What is **125 ÷ 5**?

(How many 5s go into 125?)

1. **Set it out in using the bus stop method**

$$\text{e.g. } 5\overline{\smash{)}125}$$

2. **Then go through asking the following questions:**

$$\text{e.g. } 5\overline{\smash{)}1\,2^2\!5} \quad\overset{2}{}$$

3. **How many times does 5 go into 12?**
Twice. Put a 2 on top. It has remainder 2, carry it over and bring the remainder you haven't yet used down to create a new number, 25.

$$\text{e.g. } 5\overline{\smash{)}1\,2^2\!5} \quad\overset{25}{}$$

4. **How many times does 5 go into 25?**
Five. Put a 5 on top. No remainder. As we have nothing else to divide we can stop.

So the answer is **25**.

Example 2: Test Question

The total distance of a cross country run was **27** miles. The run consisted of **4** laps around a route. How long was one lap?

$$27 \div 4$$

$$4\overline{)2^27.\ ^30\ ^20}$$

with **0 6 . 7 5** on top

27 miles ÷ 4 = 6.75 miles

Example 3: Test Question

Teachers at Forest Academy spend **135** pounds on travel. The total amount is equally split between **6** trips. What is the cost of each trip?

$$135 \div 6$$

$$6\overline{)1^13^15.\ ^30\ 0}$$

with **0 2 2 . 5** on top

£135 ÷ 6 = £22.50

2.1 I can perform division using the standard method – SKILLS Questions

Find solutions to the following, giving your answer to 2 decimal places where required.

a)	5 ÷ 4	j)	15 ÷ 9	s)	5489 ÷ 8
b)	9 ÷ 8	k)	46 ÷ 4	t)	1174 ÷ 20
c)	6 ÷ 4	l)	154 ÷ 5	u)	9949 ÷ 7
d)	4 ÷ 1	m)	156 ÷ 12	v)	1655 ÷ 60
e)	10 ÷ 10	n)	487 ÷ 20	w)	12879 ÷ 12
f)	52 ÷ 15	o)	519 ÷ 3	x)	14567 ÷ 75
g)	45 ÷ 4	p)	561 ÷ 5	y)	48765 ÷ 50
h)	95 ÷ 6	q)	498 ÷ 4	z)	14787 ÷ 125
i)	74 ÷ 8	r)	1054 ÷ 6		

2.2 I can perform division using the standard method – TEST Questions

a) The staff members at River Community School have 339.5 litres of paint. This is the total amount needed for 7 days of events at a nursery. How much paint is needed for one day?

b) A group of pupils cycle 213.5 miles in preparation for regional trials. The total distance is made up of 7 laps around the country route. What is the distance of one lap?

c) A food technology department had 192.5 litres of milk. The total volume was used during 7 days of baking. What was the volume used in one day assuming that an equal amount was used each day?

d) A school bought 138 pieces of computer equipment. The equipment is equally shared between four computer suites. How many pieces of equipment did each room get?

e) The librarian at St Cuthbert's buys three sets of books for a total of £72. Each set cost the same amount. How much does one set cost?

f) Fifteen school teachers drink a total of 30 litres of coffee during one month. How much does one teacher drink, assuming they all drink the same amount?

g) Ten pupils carry 75 kilograms of equipment. How much does each pupil carry on average?

h) The entry to a museum cost £140 for seventy pupils. How much did one ticket cost?

i) Twenty pupils carry a total of 180 kilograms worth of equipment for their school's sports day. If each pupil carries the same amount, how much does each pupil carry?

j) Ninety parents pay a total of £765 pounds for their child's school trip. How much does each parent pay?

k) Students at a school cycle 103 kilometres in a cross-country event. The total distance is made up of 2 laps around the city. What is the distance of one lap?

l) A receptionist buys 198 litres of water. The total volume is needed for 3 days' worth of exams. What is the volume needed for one day?

m) A group of students have 303 kilograms of flour which is equally shared out across 6 baking events. How much flour is needed for one baking event? Give your answer in kilograms.

n) Fifty-five students pay a total of 385 pounds for their holiday. How much does each pupil pay? Give your answer in pounds.

o) Fifteen teachers walk a total of 112.5 kilometres around a school on an open evening. How far did each teacher walk on average?

p)   If forty-five pupils carry a total of 315 kilograms worth of camping equipment and each pupil carries the same amount, how much does one pupil carry?

q)   Fifty parents make 300 cupcakes for a bring-and-buy sale. Assuming each parent baked the same number, how many does each parent bake?

r)   Fifty-five pupils drink a total of 192.5 litres of cola at a party. They all drink the same amount. How much does each pupil drink? Give your answer in litres,

s)   Eighty parents pay a total of £280 for their child's school trip. How much does one parent pay?

t)   35 pieces of stationery were shared between 5 students to ensure they had the right equipment for their maths test. How many pieces of stationery did each student receive?

u)   A group of students share 220 sweets between 44 of them. How many sweets does each student get?

v)   The maths teacher has worked out that on average eighty teachers drink a total of 720 litres of water. If they all drink the same amount of water, how much water does one teacher drink?

w)   Eighty-five parents walk a total of 212.5 kilometres on a school trip. How far does each parent walk?

x)   Fifteen teachers equally contributed 90 pounds for new exercise books. How much does each teacher pay?

y)   Thirty-five pupils eat 35 bars of chocolate in total. How many bars does each child eat, assuming they all have an equal amount?

z)   Sixty head teachers tracked their walk around a conference. In total, they covered 90 kilometres. Assume they all walked the same distance. How far did each head teacher walk?

2.3   I can solve decimal division - Introduction

The method we will use to divide decimals is explained using examples. It will require knowledge of the short division method demonstrated below.

If dividing with a decimal we need to multiply by a factor of 10 (10, 100, 1000, 10000 etc....) to get rid of the decimal- as it is easier to work with whole numbers.

Explanation Example

Example 1

What is **6 ÷ 0.5** ?

$$6 ÷ 0.5$$

1. Multiply both numbers by **10**.
2. Perform the division. So divide by 5
3. This gives the answer of 12

$$6 × 10 ÷ 0.5 × 10$$

$$60 ÷ 5$$

$$12$$

Example 2

What is **10 ÷ 0.05**?

$$10 ÷ 0.05$$

1. Multiply both numbers by **100** to make the division easier.

$$10 × 100 ÷ 0.05 × 100$$

$$1000 ÷ 5$$

$$200$$

2. Perform the division.

Example 3: Test Question

What is **0.2 ÷ 20**?

1. This example is different as the number you are dividing is a decimal.

2. Perform the division **0.2** divided by **2** which is **0.1** and then move the decimal place 1 to the left as you are dividing by **20** instead of **2**. For every extra **0** you move the decimal place by one.

$$0.2 \div 2 = 0.1$$

$$0.2 \div 20$$

$$0.01$$

Example 4: Test Question

What is **0.03 ÷ 0.9**?

1. Multiply both numbers by **10** to make the division easier.

2. Perform the division.

$$0.03 \div 0.9$$

$$0.03 \times 10 \div 0.9 \times 10$$

$$0.3 \div 9$$

$$0.033 \text{ (to 3dp)}$$

Example 5 Test Question

What is **0.01 ÷ 0.008**?

1. Multiply both numbers by **1000** to make the division easier.

2. Perform the division.

$$0.01 \div 0.008$$

$$0.01 \times 1000 \div 0.008 \times 1000$$

$$10 \div 8$$

$$1.25$$

2.4   I can solve decimal division questions – SKILLS Questions

a)	1.5 ÷ 5	j)	100 ÷ 0.8	s)	1 ÷ 0.001
b)	2.6 ÷ 3	k)	1.65 ÷ 0.3	t)	312 ÷ 1.6
c)	11.2 ÷ 4	l)	6 ÷ 0.006	u)	4158 ÷ 2.4
d)	5.5 ÷ 0.5	m)	5656 ÷ 0.8	v)	179 ÷ 64.34
e)	7.2 ÷ 0.9	n)	4 ÷ 0.0002	w)	6933 ÷ 0.003
f)	0.25 ÷ 0.05	o)	0.16 ÷ 0.16	x)	11111 ÷ 0.9
g)	16 ÷ 0.04	p)	0.7 ÷ 0.002	y)	3.145 ÷ 0.0003
h)	12.6 ÷ 1.2	q)	10 ÷ 0.25	z)	0.22 ÷ 0.07
i)	99 ÷ 0.03	r)	1 ÷ 0.7		

2.5   I can solve decimal division questions – TEST Questions

a) What is two hundred and forty-three divided by zero point zero one?

b) What is eight thousand two hundred and forty-seven divided by zero point two?

c) What is one thousand six hundred and forty-six divided by zero point two?

d) What is seven hundred and twenty-nine divided by zero point zero one?

e) What is twenty-seven thousand four hundred and thirty-five divided by zero point zero one?

f) What is fifteen thousand eight hundred and forty divided by zero point three?

g) What is one thousand two hundred and sixty-six divided by zero point one?

h) What is nine thousand forty-three divided by zero point two?

i) What is five hundred and ninety-three divided by zero point two?

j) What is six thousand one hundred and sixty-eight divided by zero point three?

k) What is two thousand three hundred and seventy-four divided by zero point two?

l) What is four thousand five hundred and sixty-seven divided by zero point one?

m) What is two hundred and forty-seven divided by zero point zero one?

n) What is three hundred and sixty-two divided by zero point one?

o) What is one hundred and thirty-two divided by zero point one?

p) What is twenty-one thousand two hundred and seventy divided by zero point three?

q) What is three hundred and two divided by zero point zero zero one?

r) What is nine hundred and eighty-seven divided by zero point one?

s) What is two thousand six hundred and fifty-one divided by zero point two?

t) What is seventeen thousand three hundred and nineteen divided by zero point zero one?

u) What is one hundred and fifty-five divided by zero point zero zero one?

v) What is four hundred and ninety-five divided by zero point three?

w) What is thirteen thousand six hundred and eighty-three divided by zero point zero one?

x) What is three thousand eight hundred and eighty-one divided by zero point two?

y) What is nine hundred and sixty-seven divided by zero point zero one?

z) What is eight thousand two hundred and sixty divided by zero point two?

3. Fractions

Introduction to simplifying fractions

Write your answer in its simplest form, are words that often appear on the skills test. This means if you have a fraction you need to write it such that the top and bottom numbers cannot be divided by the same number any further.

In the rectangle below $\frac{6}{18}$ squares have been shaded in. However we can simplify this fraction, by dividing top and bottom by 6:

This gives us $\frac{1}{3}$ which we can see is true from looking at the diagram as 1 in every 3 squares is blue.

Explanation Example

Example 1

Simplify $\frac{4}{8}$

1. Find what number you can divide 4 and 8 by.

   4

2. Divide the top by 4.

3. Divide the bottom by 4.

4. Can we divide it any further?

   No

$$\frac{4}{8} = \frac{1}{2}$$

Example 2

Simplify $\frac{66}{110}$

1. As both of these numbers are even we can divide by 2.

2. Both of these numbers aren't even. They are both divisible by 11.

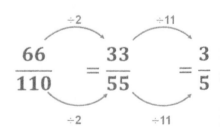

$$\frac{66}{110} = \frac{33}{55} = \frac{3}{5}$$

Example 3: Test Question

In a year with **18** students, **3** passed the English exam. What fraction of the year passed the English exam? Give your answer in its lowest terms.

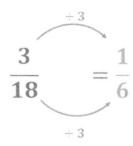

Example 4: Test Question

In a year with **45** pupils, **72** passed the English exam.

What fraction of the year did **not** pass the English exam? Give your answer in its lowest terms.

72 − 45 = 27 *didn't pass*

Need Help? Book a professional numeracy skills tutor. Visit https://www.qtsmathstutor.co.uk/ to find out more.

3.1   I can simplify fractions – SKILLS Questions

Simplify the following fractions.

a)	$\dfrac{4}{8}$	h)	$\dfrac{2}{10}$	o)	$\dfrac{18}{81}$	u)	$\dfrac{18}{42}$
b)	$\dfrac{2}{18}$	i)	$\dfrac{5}{55}$	p)	$\dfrac{16}{88}$	v)	$\dfrac{36}{156}$
c)	$\dfrac{3}{12}$	j)	$\dfrac{4}{32}$	q)	$\dfrac{27}{45}$	w)	$\dfrac{24}{84}$
d)	$\dfrac{11}{110}$	k)	$\dfrac{2}{24}$	r)	$\dfrac{25}{35}$	x)	$\dfrac{48}{50}$
e)	$\dfrac{7}{42}$	l)	$\dfrac{20}{30}$	s)	$\dfrac{60}{70}$	y)	$\dfrac{76}{80}$
f)	$\dfrac{2}{14}$	m)	$\dfrac{22}{77}$	t)	$\dfrac{132}{180}$	z)	$\dfrac{261}{270}$
g)	$\dfrac{4}{12}$	n)	$\dfrac{20}{50}$				

3.2   I can simplify fractions – TEST Questions

a)   In a class of 36 children, 9 were boys. What fraction of the class were boys? Give your answer in its lowest terms.

b)   In a gym with 350 members, only 35 were above the age of 60. What fraction of the members were below the age of 60? Give your answer in its lowest terms.

c)   In a year of 63 children, 18 passed the English exam. What fraction of the year did not pass the English exam? Give your answer in its lowest terms.

d) Eleven out of 33 pupils in a class needed additional support. What fraction of the class did not need additional support? Give your answer in its lowest terms.

e) Out of 150 pupils, 15 needed to wear glasses. What fraction of the school did not need to wear glasses? Give your answer in its lowest terms.

f) In a class of 36 pupils, 9 take part in the sports day. What fraction of the class did not take part in the sports day? Give your answer in its lowest terms.

g) In a group of 35 pupils, 15 preferred maths to English. What fraction of the group preferred English to maths? Give your answer in its lowest terms.

h) Fifty out of 750 children obtained a Grade 9 at GCSE. What proportion of the children achieved a Grade 9? Give your answer as fraction in its lowest terms.

i) In a school of 300 children, 20 students were deemed as excelling beyond their years; what fraction of the school was this? Give your answer in its lowest terms.

j) In a year with 42 pupils, 35 took part in the sports day. Writing your answer as a fraction in its simplest form, what proportion took part in the sports day?

k) In a class of 30 pupils, 10 were girls. What fraction of the class were girls? Give your answer in its lowest terms.

l)   In a year with 27 students, 3 passed the English exam. What fraction of the year did not pass the English exam? Give your answer in its lowest terms.

m)   Out of 900 students, 45 did not pass the English exam. What fraction of the school did not pass the English exam? Give your answer in its lowest terms.

n)   In a year with 18 children, 3 liked football. What fraction of the year did not like football? Give your answer in its lowest terms.

o)   On a trip of 21 pupils, 7 did not go into the museum. What fraction of the class went into the museum? Give your answer in its lowest terms.

p)   Out of 300 drinks in the school shop, 20 were sugar-free. What fraction of the drinks was not sugar-free? Give your answer in its lowest terms.

q)   Out of 60 students, 15 brought their own sandwiches. What fraction of the students did not bring sandwiches? Give your answer in its lowest terms.

r)   From a group of 45 children, 10 get detention. What fraction of the group got detention? Give your answer in its lowest terms.

s)   In a school with 700 children, 35 are in the school band. What fraction of the school is in the band? Give your answer in its lowest terms.

t) Out of 48 children taking a higher level French exam, 6 passed. What fraction of the year did not pass the French exam? Give your answer in its lowest terms.

u) In a primary school year of 50 pupils, 20 take part in the talent show. What fraction of the year takes part in the talent show? Give your answer in its lowest terms.

v) In a class of 24 pupils, 6 are awarded a merit for excellent achievements. What fraction of the class did not receive a merit? Give your answer in its lowest terms.

w) In a school there were 50 teachers, 200 girls, 20 support staff and 180 boys. What fraction of the total people in the school were teachers? Give your answer in its lowest terms.

x) In a year with 54 students, 12 took geography. What fraction of the year took geography? Give your answer in its lowest terms.

y) In a year of 35 children, 10 take part in the sports day. What fraction of the year takes part in the sports day? Give your answer in its lowest terms.

z) In a class, 8 students were late handing in their homework, 3 didn't hand in their homework at all and 13 did hand their homework in on time. What fraction of the class handed in their homework late? Give your answer in its lowest terms.

3.3   Convert between fractions, decimals and percentages
Introduction

Of the twelve mental arithmetic questions, it is likely that a conversion between fractions, decimals and percentages (FDP) will come up. It will therefore be useful to memorise some conversions and practice converting from one to the other. View some key fractions, decimals and percentages on **page 9**. Once you have learnt these, other FDP conversions can be calculated using them.

There are two different methods for completing FDP conversions:

1. You can cancel fractions down, making it easier to convert them once you have learnt the basic conversions.

2. An alternative method is to make the denominator (bottom number) equal 100, the top number will then be equal to that number as a percentage. (e.g. $\frac{57}{100} = 57\%$)

Explanation Example

Example 1: Convert $\frac{16}{20}$ into a percentage.

Example 1: Method 1

1. Cancel the fraction down by dividing the top and bottom by 4.

2. Using your knowledge of fractions. $\frac{1}{5} = 20\%$ we can then convert the result into a percentage as shown.

Using this method

$\frac{4}{5} = 80\%$

Example 1: Method 2

1. The aim of this method is to get the bottom number to 100. To do this we multiply both numbers by 5.

2. When any fraction is written with the bottom number as 100 the top number will equal the percentage. Using this we can calculate the percentage.

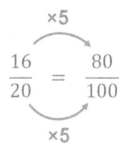

Using this method

$\frac{80}{100} = 80\%$

Example 2:

Convert 0.96 to a percentage.

1. You simply multiply by 100 to convert from a decimal into a percentage.

$$0.96 \times 100 = 96\%$$

Example 3: Test Question

In a class of 18 pupils, **12** passed the English exam. What proportion of the class failed the English exam? Give your answer as decimal.

$$\div 3$$

$$\frac{6}{18} = \frac{1}{3}$$

$$\div 3$$

$$\frac{1}{3} = 0.33$$

Example 4: Test Question

In a reception class of 25 students, **5** were performing well above average. What percentage of the class performed well above average?

$$\times 4$$

$$\frac{5}{25} = \frac{20}{100}$$

$$\times 4$$

Using your conversion knowledge

$$\frac{20}{100} = 20\%$$

3.4   I can convert between fractions, decimals and percentages – SKILLS Questions

Write each of the following fractions as a decimal and a percentage.

a) $\dfrac{1}{2}$ h) $\dfrac{1}{10}$ o) $\dfrac{3}{4}$ v) $\dfrac{4}{5}$

b) $\dfrac{1}{3}$ i) $\dfrac{1}{25}$ p) $\dfrac{2}{3}$ w) $\dfrac{24}{25}$

c) $\dfrac{1}{4}$ j) $\dfrac{1}{50}$ q) $\dfrac{68}{200}$ x) $\dfrac{1}{15}$

d) $\dfrac{1}{5}$ k) $\dfrac{3}{5}$ r) $\dfrac{24}{120}$ y) $\dfrac{5}{8}$

e) $\dfrac{1}{6}$ l) $\dfrac{4}{10}$ s) $\dfrac{6}{40}$ z) $\dfrac{4}{11}$

f) $\dfrac{1}{7}$ m) $\dfrac{3}{25}$ t) $\dfrac{9}{12}$

g) $\dfrac{1}{8}$ n) $\dfrac{16}{50}$ u) $\dfrac{3}{12}$

3.5   I can convert between fractions, decimals and percentages – TEST Questions

a)   A school's senior management team was made up of 27 people above the age of 40 and only 3 people below this age. What proportion of the senior management team was below the age of 40? Give your answer as a decimal.

b)   In a school of 150 people, 15 were teachers. What proportion of the school were not teachers? Give your answer as a percentage.

c)   In a class of 36 students, 6 of the students had brown hair. What proportion of the class did not have brown hair? Give your answer as a decimal.

d)   Two thirds of a Physical Education class selected football as their first choice of activity. What proportion did not choose football? Give your answer as a decimal.

e)   60 students were assessed for their maths ability in comparison to the national average for their age group, 15 were found to be under achieving. What proportion of the students was under achieving? Give your answer as a decimal.

f)   Out of 480 pupils, 60 needed additional support. What proportion of the group did not need additional support? Give your answer as a percentage.

g)   In a year of 150 students, 25 achieved an A* grade in their recent history exam. What proportion of the year achieved the highest grade? Give your answer as a decimal.

h)   Out of 275 students, 55 said they enjoyed Art. What proportion of the students enjoyed Art? Give your answer as a decimal.

i)   A school teacher bought pens, pencils and rulers for her class. Out of the 64 pieces of stationery she bought, 8 of them were pencils. What percentage of the stationery were pencils?

j)   From a primary school of 600 pupils, 60 take part in the sports day. What proportion of the school take part in the sports day? Give your answer as a percentage.

k) A teacher marked 60 exam papers, of which 48 were graded. What proportion of the exam papers was ungraded? Give your answers as a decimal.

l) In a year with 100 children, 50 were boys. What proportion of the year were not boys? Give your answer as a decimal.

m) From a total of 225 students, 45 opt to go on a school trip. What proportion of the group take part in the school trip? Give your answer as a decimal.

n) 55 students passed their geography assignment whilst the remaining 165 students did not. What proportion of the group passed the geography assignment? Give your answer as a percentage.

o) Staff members in a school are composed of teachers and support workers. If there are 20 support workers and 60 teachers, what proportion of the total staff are support workers? Give your answer as a decimal.

p) A year group consists of students who choose football and students who choose rugby. If 30 students choose rugby and 120 students choose football, what percentage of the year group choose football?

q) In a year of 500 children, 50 needed additional support. What proportion of the year needed additional support? Give your answer as a decimal.

r) In a class with 24 pupils, 4 passed the English exam. What proportion of the class did not pass the English exam? Give your answer as a decimal.

s) In a year group of 360 students, 60 travelled to school by car. What proportion of the year group travelled to school by car? Give your answer as a percentage.

t) In a year of 210 students, 35 were born between June and August. What proportion of the year was born between June and August? Give your answer as a percentage.

u) In a group with 440 students, 55 had their birthdays during the Autumn term. What proportion of the group had their birthdays in the Autumn term? Give your answer as a percentage.

v) In a school of 240 pupils, 40 had unacceptable levels of absence. What proportion of the school did not meet the expected attendance? Give your answer as a decimal.

w) In a year of 320 children, 40 took part in the school talent show. What proportion of the year did not take part in the talent show? Give your answer as a percentage.

x) In a school of 1000 people, 100 were teachers and staff. What proportion of the school were teachers and staff? Give your answer as a percentage.

y) In a class of 40 pupils, 4 failed their maths test. What proportion of the class failed their maths test? Give your answer as a decimal.

z) In a school of 1100 students, 110 students walked to school. What proportion of the students did not walk to school? Give your answer as a percentage.

3.6   I can calculate a fraction of an amount

Introduction

There are many proportion questions on the mental arithmetic section of the test and these can be applied to various contexts. The questions vary the proportion from fractions to decimals to percentages. We recommend taking another look at multiplying by fractions on **page 21**, multiplying decimals on **page 28** and converting between fraction, decimals and percentages on **page 50**.

Note: the word **of** in mathematics means × **(times)**.

Explanation Example

Example 1

Find $\frac{2}{5}$ of 20.

1. Splitting 20 into fifths gives us 4.
2. Therefore one fifth is 4.
3. Find $\frac{2}{5}$ of 20.

The method is: divide by the bottom of the fraction (denominator) and times by the top (numerator).

$\frac{1}{5}$ of 20

$20 \div 5 \times 1 = 4$

$\frac{2}{5}$ of 20

$20 \div 5 \times 2 = 8$

Example 2

Find 40% of 60.

1. Find 10% by dividing the amount by 10.
2. Find 40% by multiplying 6 by 4.

$10\% = 60 \div 10 = 6$

$40\% = 4 \times 10\% = 4 \times 6 = 24$

40% of 60 is 24

Example 3

Find 0.25 of 20.

Convert this to the fraction $\frac{1}{4}$ or a percentage 25% and use the method you feel most comfortable with.

$$20 \div 4 \times 1 = 5$$

0.25 of 20 = 5

Example 4: Test Question

In a class with **40** pupils, $\frac{2}{10}$ passed their English exam. How many people in the class passed their English exam?

$$40 \div 10 = 4$$

$$4 \times 2 = 8$$

8 pupils passed the English exam

Example 5: Test Question

The total cost of a coach for a school trip came to **140** pounds, **25%** was charged to the parents. How much did the parents pay?

$$25\% = \frac{1}{4}$$

$$\frac{1}{4} \text{ of } 140$$

$$140 \div 4 = 35$$

25% of 140 is £35

Note: Fraction of an amount questions are given in section 1.7 on **page 24.**

Note: Fraction of an amount questions are given in section 1.7 on **page 24.**

3.7   I can calculate a proportion of an amount - SKILLS Questions

a) 45% of 175

b) 80% of 65

c) 0.05 of 325

d) 15% of 565

e) 0.65 of 400

f) 40% of 650

g) 45% of 740

h) 0.25 of 780

i) 0.15 of 330

j) 0.35 of 575

k) 0.85 of 255

l) 0.6 of 455

m) 0.9 of 405

n) 50% of 15

o) 40% of 595

p) 75% of 360

q) 60% of 285

r) 40% of 955

s) 0.1 of 965

t) 0.85 of 920

u) 70% of 680

v) 60% of 490

w) 0.65 of 240

x) 25% of 95

y) 0.1 of 65

z) 0.6 of 620

3.8   I can calculate a proportion of an amount – TEST Questions

a) In a class with 24 pupils, $\frac{1}{3}$ took part in the sports day. How many pupils in the class did not take part in the sports day?

b) In a year group with 150 students, 10% passed their English exam. What number of the year group did not pass the English exam?

c) The total cost of the school trip was £350, 10% was charged to the parents. How much does the school contribute? Give your answer in pounds.

d) In a group with 60 pupils, $\frac{1}{4}$ could play an instrument. What number of the group could not play an instrument?

e) New instruments cost 160 pounds, 12.5% of the cost is due to shipping. How much of the cost is not due to shipping?

f) A school fun day cost 480 pounds. $\frac{1}{8}$ of the cost was covered by donations. How much did the school fun day cost after the donations were deducted?

g) In a school with 700 students, 10% passed the annual maths bonanza quiz. How many pupils is this?

h) A school organised a coach to take children to weekly swimming lessons. The coach cost £75 pounds. $\frac{1}{3}$ of the cost was covered by the school. How much did the school pay?

i) In a class of 50 students 10% needed additional support. What number of the class needed additional support?

j) A theme park ticket cost 60 pounds, $\frac{1}{3}$ of this cost was for queue jump. How much of the ticket cost was due to queue jump?

k) The new sports kits cost 160 pounds each. 25% of the cost is for the school branding. How much of the kit cost is not due to the school branding?

l) The library books annual book purchase totalled 440 pounds. $\frac{1}{8}$ of the cost was due to tax. How much of the book purchase was not due to tax?

m) In a year with 330 children, $\frac{1}{6}$ of the children spent the day off site. How many children is this?

n) In a class of 14 students, 50% hand their homework in on time. How many people did not hand their homework in on time?

o) A new microscope lens costs 90 pounds. $\frac{1}{6}$ of the cost was due to protective packaging, the rest was for the lens itself. What was the cost of just the lens?

p) The weekly school milk bill was 210 pounds. $\frac{1}{5}$ of the bill was for full-fat milk. What was the cost of the milk that was not full-fat, assuming all milk cost the same amount?

q) The cake sale raised 135 pounds. $\frac{1}{3}$ of the income came from chocolate cake. How much money did not come from chocolate cake?

r) In a year of 550 children, 10% achieved a Grade 5. How many children in the year did not achieve a Grade 5?

s) The school trip cost £30, 50% was for museum entry. How much did museum entry cost?

t) In a class with 15 students, 20% are picked for the school football team. How many students from this class play for the school football team?

u) At Bloomsbury High, there were 100 children in year 7 and 50% were girls. How many girls were there in year 7?

v) A new school door cost £360. $\frac{1}{6}$ of this cost was due to fitting and the rest was the cost of the door. How much did the door cost without fitting?

w) In a year with 600 pupils, $\frac{2}{5}$ opted in for revision lessons. How many pupils in the year did not attend revision lessons?

x) In a school with 330 children, $\frac{1}{6}$ will move school at the end of the year. What number of children will move school?

y) In a group of 10 pupils, 50% wear glasses. How many pupils do not wear glasses?

z) In a school of 400 pupils, 25% can play an instrument. How many pupils can play an instrument?

4. Percentage increase and decrease

Introduction

If you can find the percentage of an amount then percentage increase and decrease is very simple. If it is increase you add it on and if it is decrease you take it away. For example, 20 increased by 10% is 22 and 20 decreased by 10% is 18.

Explanation Example

Example 1

Increase 50 by 10%.

1. Find 10%.
2. Increase means add it on.

$$10\% = 50 \div 10 = 5$$
$$50 + 10\% = 50 + 5 = 55$$

Example 2

Decrease 40 by 40%.

1. Find 40%.
2. Decrease means take it away.

$$10\% = 40 \div 10 = 4$$
$$40\% = 10\% \times 4 = 4 \times 4 = 16$$
$$40 - 40\% = 40 - 16 = 24$$

Example 3

Decrease 25 by 5%.

1. Find 5%.
2. Decrease means take it away.

$$10\% = 25 \div 10 = 2.5$$
$$5\% = 10\% \div 2 = 2.5 \div 2 = 1.25$$
$$25 - 5\% = 25 - 1.25 = 23.75$$

Example 4: Test Question

A teacher stretches a **125** millimetre spring *increasing* its size by **75%**. What is the new size of the spring?

$$10\% = 125 \div 10 = 12.5$$
$$70\% = 12.5 \times 7 = 87.5$$
$$5\% = 10\% \div 2 = 12.5 \div 2 = 6.25$$
$$75\% = 87.5 + 6.25 = 93.75$$
$$125 + 93.25 = 218.75\text{mm}$$

Example 5: Test Question

A teacher freezes an **80** centimetre elastic band *decreasing* its size by **81%**. What is the new size of the elastic band?

$$10\% = 80 \div 10 = 8$$
$$80\% = 8 \times 8 = 64$$
$$1\% = 10\% \div 10 = 0.8$$
$$81\% = 64 + 0.8 = 64.8$$
$$80 - 64.8 = 15.2 \text{ cm}$$

4.1 I can calculate percentage increase and decrease – TEST Questions

a) A train operator decreases the price on a £30 return ticket by 5%. How much discount does he give?

b) A primary school with 100 students increases its capacity by 85%. How many students are now able to attend the primary school?

c) A drama class of 50 increases in size by 66%. How many people are now in the drama class?

d) 60 teachers attend a union meeting. This number declines by 5% at the next meeting. How many teachers were there at the next union meeting?

e) A council's school budget increases from 45 million pounds by 90% to enable a region wide school building programme. How much is the council's school budget now?

f) A student breaks a 45-centimetre ruler decreasing its size by 20%. What is the new size of the ruler?

g) A £15 dress in a sale has 25% knocked off its marked price with the use of student discount. What is the new price of the dress?

h) A council estimates that a class of 25 pupils will have increased by 76% in the year 2040. What will be the size of the class in 2040?

i) A trailer contains 120kg of cargo. This is then increased by 35% following a pickup. What is the new weight of the cargo?

j) A teacher runs an after school sports club containing 95 students. The teacher intends to expand the club by increasing the number of places by 60%. How many places are there available in the new class?

k) A teacher freezes a 45 centimetre piece of material decreasing its size by 41%. What is the new size of the piece of material?

l) A shop decreases the price on a £110 pound suit by 76%. What is the new cost of the suit?

m) A student stretches an 80-centimetre spring increasing its size by 70%. What is the new size of the spring?

n) A £15 watch gets scratched, decreasing its value by 45%. What is the new value of the watch?

o) The English department's printing budget is increased by 11% from £55 per term. What is their new printing budget?

p) The normal size of the drama group, which is 85 is expected to increase by 45% following a well-reviewed production. What will be the new size of the drama group?

q) One £100 talent show ticket has its cost decreased by 5% if you book in advance. What is the cost of the talent show ticket if you book early?

r) Rocketing wholesale prices increase the cost of a £25 barrel of oil by 76%. What is the new cost of the oil?

s) Increase 45 by 80%.

t) A schools £950 stationery budget is set to increase by 70% to help accommodate many additional students. How much will the school now get to spend on stationery?

u) A primary school is set to expand drastically in size and therefore it will have capacity to take in new students. The number of students increases by 100%. How many students will there be if originally there was 85?

v) Inspectors stretch a 95m safety rope increasing its size by 90% before it snaps. What size is the rope just before it snaps?

w) Increase 45mm by 65%.

x) A food shop used to cost £75 but now it costs 16% more. How much does it now cost?

y) Adding nitrogen to a 50cm plant will cause its size to increase by 36% in one season. What will the size of the plant be by the end of one season?

z) A student discovers a 55-millimetre elastic band can increase in size by 20% before it snaps. At what size will the band snap?

5. Conversions (and Ratios)

Introduction

Conversion questions come up in many different scenarios within the skills test. Two common types of conversion questions are based on currency and distance, which is what the test questions in this section will focus on.

To work through the conversion method you need to be comfortable with the fact that equations need to be balanced. By this, we mean, whatever you do to one side of the equation you have to do to the other. Imagine a set of scales with 10kg on one side and five lots of 2kg on the other. The scales are balanced. Provided we perform the same calculation to both sides, such as multiplying by 2, they will remain balanced. Both sides are now 20kg. Equations follow the same rule.

5.1   Conversion Method

Explanation Example

Example 1:

If 5 bananas cost £1, how much will 6 bananas cost?

1. We can work out the cost of one banana by dividing both sides of the equation by 5. This gives us the result of £0.20 or 20p per banana.

2. We then multiply the left hand side by six to give us six bananas.

3. Then we do the same to the right hand side. Six multiplied by 20p is £1.20.

What we know

5 bananas = £1

÷5   ÷5

1 banana = £.0.20

×6   ×6

6 bananas = £1.20

What we know

Example 2 | Currency | Test Question

The exchange rate is £1 to $1.50. You have £100, how many dollars will you get?

1. Write what we know and what we want.

2. What do we multiply 1 by to get 100?

$$100 \div 1 = 100$$

3. Multiply both sides by 100.

$$1.50 \times 100 = 150$$

What we know

£1 = $1.50

× 100   × 100

£100 = $150

What we want

Example 3 | Currency | Test Question

The exchange rate is £1 to €0.80. You have £25, how many euros will you get?

1. Write what we know and what we want.
2. What do we multiply by?
   25
3. Multiply both sides by the same.

$$0.80 \times 25 = 20$$

What we know

£1 = €0.80

× 25   × 25

£25 = €20

What we want

Example 4 | Distance | Test Question

A bus travelled 320 km. Miles to km is calculated in the ratio 5: 8.

How many miles did the bus travel?

1. Write what we know and what we want.

2. We don't know the multiplier. We can work it out. What do we multiply the right by?

   40

3. Therefore, multiplying the left by 40 gives us 200

What we know

5 miles = 8 km

× 40   × 40

200 miles = 320 km

What we want

Example 5 | Ratio | Test Question

A sauce has the ingredients butter and flour in the ratio 3:5.

If you measure 150g of flour, how much butter do you need?

1. Write what we know and what we want.

2. We don't know the multiplier. The multiplier is 30 (relationship on right).

3. Multiplying the left by 30, 90g butter.

What we know

3 butter : 5 Flour

× 40   × 40

90g butter : 150g Flour

What we want

5.2   I can convert between currencies and distances – TEST Questions

a)   On a trip to the USA, each person received $336. How many pounds did each person exchange assuming £1 pound is equal to $1.4?

b)   A class went to China, each person exchanged 680 pounds. What is this in Yuan assuming £1 is equal to ¥1.3?

c)   During a tour of Asia, the accommodation cost 660 pounds. How many Yuan did the accommodation cost if 1 pound is equal to ¥1.1?

d)   A school went on a trip to France. Knowing 1 pound is equal to 1.2 Euros and each person took 1080 pounds. How many Euros did each person receive?

e)   A class went to Japan, the trip cost 1060 pounds. How many yen did the trip cost each person, if 1 pound is equal to 1.8 yen?

f)   A language class went to Spain. Assuming £1 is equal to €1.4 and the accommodation cost €168, how many pounds did each member of the class have to exchange?

g)   Mrs Smith went on holiday to Sweden. If 1 pound is equal to 1.9 Euros and she spent 722 euros, how many pounds did she spend?

h)   For a tour across China each person swapped £220 to begin with before exchanging an additional £220. How many Yuan did each person swap altogether, given that £1 is equal to ¥1.9?

i)   If 1 pound to 1.7 Euros is the exchange rate, what would a family holiday of four people cost each person if the total holiday cost was 1680 pounds. Give your answer in euros.

j)   1 pound exchanges to 1.1 Euros. Molly and Alice visited their grandparents in Germany, the total amount they exchanged was 520 pounds. How many Euros did they receive?

k)   Belgium was the location of this year's history trip. The accommodation cost 1000 pounds per student. Using the conversion £1:€1.2, calculate the cost of the accommodation in euros?

l)   A conference took place in Korea. If £1 is equal to ¥1.4 and the total amount exchanged was £560. How many Korean won were exchanged in total?

m)   Two teachers went to Canada. The total amount they exchanged was £720. How many dollars were exchanged in total taking £1 as $1.9?

n)   Jack's family holidayed in the USA. Taking 1 pound as 1.4 dollars and each person exchanged 300 pounds. How many dollars did each person receive?

o)   The total distance travelled on a school trip was 1560 kilometres. Using the conversion of eight kilometres to five miles, work out the total distance of the school trip in miles.

p)   A sponsored cycle in Canada ends at Toronto after covering a distance of 944 kilometres. How many miles is this sponsored cycle assuming eight kilometres is equal to five miles?

q)   Convert 1104 kilometres into miles. You may assume that 1 kilometre is $\frac{5}{8}$ of a mile.

r) The school trip will come to an end after covering 445 miles. How many kilometres is this if eight kilometres is equal to five miles?

s) Heather's tyres will need replacing after covering a distance of 376 kilometres. Using a conversion rate of eight kilometres is five miles; calculate the number of miles travelled before the tyres will need to be replaced.

t) A tour through the USA starts at Seattle and will cover 264 kilometres. How many miles is this tour if eight kilometres is equal to five miles?

u) A school bus travels 5 miles from Stop A to Stop B. This journey is completed 5 times a week. Given that 5 miles is equal to 8 kilometres, how many kilometres did the bus travel in a week?

v) A bike race in the USA ends in Chicago after covering a distance of 888 kilometres. How many miles is this bike race using a conversion rate of eight kilometres to five miles?

w) A sponsored cycle in Spain starts in Madrid and will cover 100 miles. How many kilometres is this sponsored cycle assuming eight kilometres is equal to five miles?

x) A trip around the UK starts in Oxford and has a distance of 656 kilometres. How many miles is this trip if eight kilometres is equal to five miles?

y) A family trip around Greece starts in Athens and has a distance of 415 miles. How many kilometres is this trip if eight kilometres is equal to five miles?

z) A flight across the USA has a distance of 245 miles. How many kilometres is this flight if eight kilometres is equal to five miles?

5.3   I can simplify and divide into ratios

Introduction

Ratio questions are a common feature in the numeracy skills test. You have to be able to work with ratios and simplify them into their lowest form. You can treat ratios in a similar way to conversions, what you do to one side you must do to the other. The following example shows how a ratio is simplified.

Explanation Example

Example 1

Simplify the ratio **3 : 9**.

1. What number divides into **3** and **9**?

    3

2. Divide both sides by **3**.

If we had men : women in the ratio **3 : 9** that's the same as 1 man to every three women.

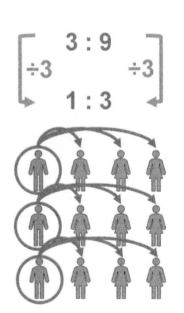

Example 2

Simplify the ratio **33 : 99**.

1. What number divides into **33** and **99**?

   33

2. Divide both sides by **33**.

3. The answer is **1:3**

$$33 : 99$$
$$\div 33 \qquad \div 33$$
$$1 : 3$$

Example 3

Divide **500** into the ratio **10 : 8 : 7**.

1. How many parts are there in total?

   25

2. How much does one part get?

   20

3. Multiply each part of the ratio by this amount.

$$10 : 8 : 7$$

$$10 + 8 + 7 = 25$$
$$500 \div 25 = 20$$

$$10 : 8 : 7$$
$$\times 20 \quad \times 20 \quad \times 20$$
$$200 : 160 : 140$$

Example 4: Test Question

A trip is planned for **24 students**. Every **8 students** must be accompanied by **2 adults**. How many **adults** are there on this trip?

$$8 : 2$$
$$\times 3 \qquad \times 3$$
$$24 : 6$$

In total there are 6 adults

Example 5: Test Question

A booklet project requires **27 white pages** to **3 blue pages**.

If there are **180 pages in total**, how many **blue pages** are there?

$$27 : 3$$
30 parts in total
$$180 \div 30 = 6$$
6 lots of 30
6 lots of blue pages
$$6 \times 3 = 18$$
18 blue pages

5.4   I can simplify and divide ratios – TEST Questions

a) In a school there are 48 full time teaching staff. For every 2 full time teachers there is 1 part time teacher or teaching assistant. How many part time teachers and teaching assistants are there in total?

b) For each pupil in a school there are 3 exercise books allocated. If the school requires 450 exercise books, how many pupils are there?

c) In a special needs school, rules state that for every 6 students there must be 2 members of staff. If there are 16 people in total, how many staff members are there?

d) At the museum, 6 students must be accompanied by 2 adults. If there are 72 students, how many people are there in total?

e) Every 5 classrooms must have at least 4 fire extinguishers There are 25 classrooms. What is the minimum number of fire extinguishers required?

f) A booklet project requires 27 white pages to 3 blue pages. If there are 90 pages in total, how many of the pages are blue?

g) An experiment is planned for 24 students. Every 8 students must be accompanied by 3 demonstrators. How many demonstrators are there for this experiment?

h) Every 6 students share 2 revision worksheets. If there is 42 students in total how many revision worksheets will there be?

i) On a school rugby tour, for every 6 students 3 rugby balls are given out to practice with. If there is 48 students in total, how many rugby balls will there be?

j) For every 18ml of water there must be 2ml of juice. In an 80ml mixture of juice and water, what is the volume of water?

k) Every 5 classrooms must have at least 5 teachers. There are 45 classrooms, what is the minimum number of teachers required?

l) A booklet requires 16 thin paper pages for every 2 thick paper pages. The finished booklet is 144 pages long, how many thick pages are there?

m) A trip to London Zoo is planned for 20 students. Given that every 5 students get 2 maps to share, how many maps are given out to the student's altogether?

n) In a shop, on average, every 6 children purchase a drink. On a Monday morning, if there are 12 children who visit the shop in total, how many drinks can the shopkeeper expect to sell?

o)   For every 18 students who passed the year 10 maths test, 3 students failed. If 54 students passed, how many students failed?

p)   At the bowling alley every 6 games purchased results in 3 free games. If 72 games are purchased, how many games are given for free?

q)   Every 2 classrooms must have at least 4 windows. There are 8 classrooms, what is the minimum number of windows you would expect to see?

r)   A display requires 21 gold stars for every 3 silver stars. If there are 120 stars altogether, how many of them are silver?

s)   An exam is to be taken by 48 students who require special attention. For every 6 students there is 3 support staff. How many support staff will the school need for the exam?

t)   For every ten additional students a school takes in over its allocated numbers it receives an additional funding point. If 13 funding points were awarded to a school, how many additional students did they take in?

u)   A reduction in the school budget means a teacher purchases two text books for every three students. If there are 33 students in the class, how many text books will be required?

v)   Every 4 drinks bought came with 2 free drinks. If 28 drinks are bought, how many drinks are given for free?

w)   In a packet of biscuits, 12 of them are coconut and 6 chocolate. The family packet has the same proportions and there are 54 biscuits in total. How many chocolate biscuits would you expect?

x) A cake requires 4 parts dried mix to 2 parts wet ingredients. In a cake of 36 parts dried mix, how many wet ingredients are needed?

y) An event is planned for 36 dogs. Every group of 4 dogs must be accompanied by 3 handlers. How many handlers are needed at this event?

z) A trip is planned for 16 students. Every group of 4 students must be accompanied by 3 adults. How many people in total are there on this trip?

6. Time

Introduction

The problem with time is there is a temptation to assume that you're working with decimal numbers which come in blocks of 10 and 100 rather than blocks of 60. There is a natural temptation to say that 0.25 of an hour is 25 minutes, whereas, 0.25 of an hour is the same as one quarter of an hour, which is 15 minutes.

We recommend making sure you are completely comfortable with your conversions between fractions and decimals, on **page 50**, as these play an important role in the conversion of decimals to minutes.

Explanation Example

Example 1

The game starts at 15:00 and lasts for 105 minutes. At what time does it end?

1. How many whole hours are there in 105 minutes?
2. Work out how many minutes are left over?
3. Add on the hours then the minutes to 15:00.

105 minutes

1 hour = 60

2 hours = 120

Therefore, 1 whole hour (60m).

105 − 60 = 45m

15:00 + 01:00 = 16:00

16:00 + 00:45 = 16:45

The game ends at 16:45

Example 2: Test Question

The event starts at 19:00 and lasts for 215 minutes. At what time does it end?

1. How many whole hours are there in 215 minutes?
2. Work out how many minutes are left over?
3. Add on the hours then the minutes to 19:00.

215 minutes

1 hour = 60

2 hours = 120

3 hours = 180

Therefore, 3 whole hours.

215 − 180 = 35m

19:00 + 03:00 = 22:00

22:00 + 00:35 = 22:35

The event ends at 22:35

Example 3: Test Question

The day starts at 09:00 and lasts for 365 minutes. At what time does it end? Give your answer in am/pm.

1. How many whole hours are there in 365 minutes?
2. Work out how many minutes are left over?
3. Add on the hours then the minutes to 09:00.
4. Convert to pm by taking away 12.

365 minutes

1h = 60, 2h = 120, 3h = 180, 4h= 240, 5h= 300, 6h= 360

Therefore, 6 whole hours.

365 – 360 = 5m

09:00 + 06:00 = 15:00

15:00 + 00:05 = 15:05

15:05 – 12:00 = 03:05pm

The day ends at 3:05pm

Example 4: Test Question

The picnic ends at 13:25 after lasting 85 minutes. At what time did it start?

1. How many whole hours are there in 85 minutes?
2. Work out how many minutes are left over?
3. Subtract the hours then the minutes from 13:25.

85 minutes

1h = 60, 2h = 120, 3h = 180, 4h= 240, 5h= 300, 6h= 360

Therefore, 1 whole hour.

85 – 60 = 25m

13:25 – 01:00 = 12:25

12:25 - 00:25 = 12:00

The picnic started at 12:00

Example 5: Test Question

The day starts at 09:00. There are 3 lessons of 50 minutes and 1 break of 15 minutes before lunch. What time does lunch start?

1. How many minutes do we have to add in total?

2. How many hours are in 165 minutes?

3. Work out how many minutes are left over?

4. Add the hours then the minutes to 09:00.

$50 \times 3 = 150$

$150 + 15 = 165$

1h = 60, 2h = 120, 3h = 180

2 whole hours.

$165 - 120 = 45m$

$09:00 + 02:00 = 11:00$

$11:00 + 00:45 = 11:45$

Lunch starts at 11:45.

6.1   I can solve problems that involve time – TEST Questions

a) A presentation ends at 11.15am after lasting for 55 minutes. This is followed by 3 speeches each lasting 55 minutes. At what time does the day finish?

b) Two students both submit an art project. One student spends 5 hours and 25 minutes on the project whilst the other spends 2 hours and 50 minutes. What is the difference between the students in the time spent completing the project?

c) A student union meeting starts at 10.00am and lasts for 30 minutes. Due to unforeseen circumstances the meeting overruns by 2 minutes. This is followed by 2 additional meetings each lasting 50 minutes. At what time does the day end?

d) A student helpline is open for 5 hours 50 minutes on a Saturday, Tuesday, Thursday and Wednesday and 6 hours 40 minutes on a Sunday and Friday. In total, for how many hours does the helpline open?

e) A sports event starts at 11.30am and lasts for 25 minutes. This is followed by 5 training sessions each lasting 40 minutes. At what time does the sports event finish?

f) A welcome session ends at 4.30pm after lasting for 35 minutes. This is following 2 information sessions each lasting 5 minutes. At what time does the day start?

g) The computer backup system runs for 3 hours 50 minutes on a Saturday and Thursday and 5 hours 40 minutes on a Tuesday, Friday and Monday. In one week, how many hours and minutes is this?

h) In a typical week a reception is staffed for 3 hours 30 minutes on a Monday and Tuesday and 5 hours a day for the remaining weekdays. How many hours is the reception staffed in a typical week?

i) A student library opens for 2 hours 10 minutes on a Monday and 7 hours 20 minutes for the rest of the days of the week except Sunday when it is closed. How long does the library open for each week? Give your answer in hours and minutes.

j) A student helpdesk opens for 6 hours 20 minutes for 3 days a week. In any given week, how many hours does the helpdesk open?

k) A school governors' meeting starts at 10.45am and lasts for 25 minutes. This is followed by 6 one-to-one sessions each lasting 55 minutes. At what time does the meeting draw to a close?

l) A teacher training morning starts at 9.45am and lasts for 86 minutes. At what time does the training finish?

m) A welcome session starts at 1.45pm and lasts for 50 minutes. This is followed by 9 information sessions each lasting 30 minutes. At what time does the day end?

n) A student spends 3 hours 25 minutes revising maths and double this length of time revising English. How long does the student spend revising overall?

o) A parent's meeting ends at 5.00pm after lasting for 45 minutes. This is following 8 sessions each lasting 20 minutes. At what time did the parents meeting start?

p) A school break starts at 11.00am and lasts for 10 minutes. This is followed by 9 GCSE study periods each lasting 35 minutes. At what time does this revision day finish?

q) A teacher training day starts at 11.30am with an introductory session that lasts for 40 minutes. This is followed by 6 lessons each lasting 60 minutes. At what time does the teacher training day finish?

r) A school play starts at 6.00pm and lasts for 50 minutes. This is followed by a round of refreshments lasting 15 minutes and a Q&A session lasting 10 minutes. At what time did the Q&As finish?

s) Two students complete a race. One student takes 4 minutes and 35 seconds to complete the race and the other takes 6 minutes and 5 seconds. What is the difference in their times? Give your answer in minutes and seconds.

t) A presentation starts at 9.00am and lasts for 35 minutes. This is followed by 10 different breakout sessions lasting 25 minutes. At what time does the day end?

u) A student spends 3 hours 15 minutes each week playing guitar, 2 hours and 20 minutes playing football and 1 hour 30 minutes playing rugby. What is the total duration of this student's extracurricular activities?

v) A teacher spends 3 hours marking year 7 classwork, 2 hours and 35 minutes marking year 10 mock exams and 1 hour 55 minutes marking year 11 homework. How long does the teacher spend marking altogether?

w) A teacher training day starts at 9.30am with a meeting which lasts for 20 minutes. This is followed by 4 training sessions each lasting 60 minutes. At what time does the teacher training day finish?

x) A debating society evening starts at 6.00pm with an introduction that lasts for 50 minutes. This is followed by 4 rounds of talks each lasting 40 minutes. At what time does the evening end?

y) A student spends 2 hours on maths homework, 35 minutes on English and 1 hour 45 minutes on French homework. How much time does the student spend doing homework?

z) A school fun day starts at 11.45am with the initial event lasting for 50 minutes. This is followed by 2 more events each lasting 60 minutes. At what time is the fun day complete?

7. Shapes

Introduction

More shape questions have started appearing in the skills test since 2018. These questions include area, perimeter and volume and they rely on the arithmetic skills you have practised earlier on in this book.

Explanation Example

Example 1

Calculate the perimeter and area of a rectangle with length 4cm and width 3cm.

1. The perimeter is the distance around the outside. This can also be calculated by 2 times the length plus 2 times the width.

2. The area is the number of 1cm^2 blocks there are inside. This can be calculated by multiplying the length by the width.

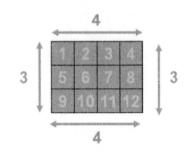

Perimeter = 4 + 3 + 4 + 3
= 14cm

Perimeter = (2 × 4) + (2 × 3) = 14cm

Area = 12cm^2

Units for area are always squared

Area = 4 × 3 = 12cm^2

Example 2

Calculate the perimeter and area of a rectangle with length 8cm and width 2cm.

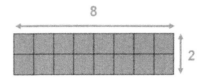

1. The perimeter is calculated by 2 times the length plus 2 times the width.

2. The area is calculated by multiplying the length by the width.

Perimeter = (2 × 8) + (2 × 2) = 16 + 4 = 20cm

Area = 8 × 2 = 16cm²

Units for area are always squared

Example 3

Calculate the volume of a cuboid with length 4cm, width 2cm and depth 3cm.

Method 1

We can also calculate the volume by multiplying the width, length and depth together.

$$2 \times 4 \times 3 = 24 \, cm^3$$

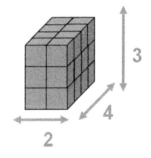

Volume = 24 cm³

Units for volume are always cubed

Example 4: Test Question

A book in a library has a width of **30** cm and a length of **45** cm. What is the perimeter of the book?

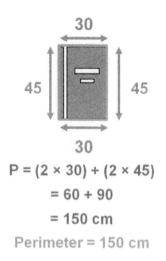

$$P = (2 \times 30) + (2 \times 45)$$
$$= 60 + 90$$
$$= 150 \text{ cm}$$

Perimeter = 150 cm

Example 5: Test Question

A large train station building has a width of **80m**, a length of **450m** and a ceiling height of **5m**. What is the volume of the train station building?

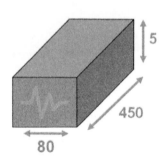

$$V = 80 \times 5 \times 450 = 400 \times 450$$

×	400	50	
400	160,000	20,000	180,000

Volume = 180,000 m³

7.1 I can calculate perimeter, area and volume – TEST Questions

a) A book in a library has a width of 35 cm and a length of 40 cm. Calculate its perimeter.

b) A shredder in the schools admin office measures 160 cm by 500 cm by 70 cm. What is the volume of the shredder?

c) A poster for the wall has a width of 80 cm and a length of 120 cm. What is the area of the poster?

d) Four tables are positioned adjacent to each other, forming a single shape. Each table measures 75 cm by 100 cm. What is the area of one table?

e) Two rooms in a school have their carpet tiles replaced. Each room has a width of 40 m and a length of 40 m. What is the total area of floor that needs carpet tiles replacing?

f) A plastic tub has a width of 160 cm, a length of 300 cm and a depth of 80 cm. What is the volume of the plastic tub?

g) A packing box at a school measures 70 cm by 300 cm by 100 cm. What is the volume of the packing box?

h) What is the area of a playing field which has a width of 65 m and a length of 290 m?

i)   A packing box at a primary school measures 40 cm by 450 cm by 40 cm. What is the volume of the packing box?

j)   A playing field at a school has a width of 70 m and a length of 220 m. What is the perimeter of the field?

k)   Two books are placed next to each other so that they form a single shape. Each measures 35 mm by 35 mm. What is the perimeter around both books?

l)   A rectangular whiteboard measures 80 cm by 95 cm. What is the area of the whiteboard?

m)   A table in the school office measures 20 cm by 200 cm by 90 cm. What is the volume of the table?

n)   A plastic tub in the school canteen has a width of 130 cm, a length of 50 cm and a depth of 20 cm. What is the volume of the plastic tub?

o)   A piece of card has a length of 40 cm and a width of 45 cm. What is the area of this piece of card?

p)   A playground needs resurfacing. It has a length of 200 m and a width of 60 m. What is the total area that needs recovering?

q)   A packing box in a hospital measures 160 cm by 500 cm by 60 cm. What is the volume of the packing box?

r)   A school hall has a width of 85 m and a length of 70 m. What is the area of the hall?

s)   What is the area of a carpet tile that measures 45 cm by 50 cm?

t)   A display in a school measures 80 cm by 105 cm. What's the perimeter of the display?

u)   A welcome mat in a reception has a width of 70 cm and a length of 105 cm. What is the area covered by this mat?

v)   A photocopier at a school has a width of 140 cm, a length of 50 cm and a depth of 40 cm. What is the volume of the photocopier?

w)   Two books are placed next to each other so that the length of each book touches. Each has a width of 30 cm and a length of 50 cm. What area is covered by both books?

x)   A classroom at a primary school measures 15 m by 5m by 2 m. What is the volume of the classroom?

y)   A football pitch measures 40 m to the half way line and is 20 m wide. What is the perimeter of the entire pitch?

z)   One playing field measures 95 m by 145 m. What is its area?

QTS MATHS TUTOR
WWW.QTSMATHSTUTOR.CO.UK

 Based on hundreds of reviews on

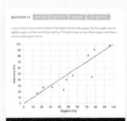
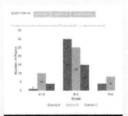
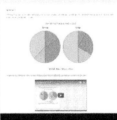

QTS LITERACY TUTOR
WWW.LITERACYSKILLSTEST.CO.UK

 Based on hundreds of reviews on

FREE ONLINE LITERACY SKILLS TEST
EXPERT 1 TO 1 TUITION WITH OUR QTS SPECIALISTS

--- **WHAT QTS LITERACY TUTOR HAS TO OFFER** ---

Spelling Practice

Punctuation Questions

Grammar Section

Comprehension Resources

Practice Tests

Expert Tutors

Correct Format

New Question Formats

Visit www.literacyskillstest.co.uk to take a Free Full Practice Test today.

10
LITERACY SKILLS TESTS

97%
LEARNER PASS RATE

490
TEST QUESTIONS

Written Data Section (Calculator Allowed)

In the written data part of the exam you will come across many different question types that look to present data in various formats. You are permitted to use a calculator in the second part of the test which is composed of 16 questions, most of which require multiple calculations.

QTS Maths Tutor has created an online calculator which mimics the calculator that you have to use in the real exam. It does take a while to get comfortable using the calculator so we recommend that you practise using it. You can access the calculator at: www.QTSmathstutor.co.uk/calculator/

The methods and techniques learnt in the mental arithmetic part of this book will help you to determine what calculations you need to make in order to get to the right answer; however there are also a lot of additional skills to learn such as how to read box plots and cumulative frequency curves amongst other things.

In this part of the book each area of the written data section of the numeracy skills test will be covered with explanations and examples to help you revise effectively. To practise questions in the onscreen exam format like the actual test we recommend you visit the QTS Maths Tutor website.

8. Using the Calculator

This section covers many of the topics covered in the mental arithmetic section. However this time you will have the aid of a calculator. As a result of this the emphasis is shifted away from your ability to perform the calculation, and onto your ability to spot which type of calculation you need to perform, whether it be multiplication, division, etc.

We recommend you refresh yourself on Section 1 Multiplication on **page 12**, section 2 Division on **page 34** and Section 5 Conversions on **page 66** before continuing.

8.1   I can perform multiplication using a calculator

Explanation Example

Each year Birdholme Avenue Academy buy 9600 workbooks, which cost £0.01 per page. Each book contains 90 pages. 1000 books can fit in one box; each box comes with a shipping charge of £4.95. How much will the total bill be?

First we need to calculate the total number of pages in all 9600 books.

$$9600 \times 90 = 864000 \text{ pages}$$

Next we need to calculate the cost for all these pages.

$$864000 \times £0.01 = £8640$$

Finally we need to add on the postage. The question says it is £4.95 for each 1000 books posted. We have 9600 books so this will mean we need 10 boxes.

$$10 \times £4.95 = £49.5$$

Adding the shipping and book costs together gives the final answer:

$$£49.5 + £8640 = £8689.50$$

a)   A teacher plans a school trip, which includes 8 adults and 22 children. Each person going on the trip must pay £87 for food and accommodation and an additional cost for entrance to the museum. Adults are charged at £7.95 and children at £4.95. What is the total cost of the trip?

b)   A head teacher must travel from School A to School B which are a distance of 14 miles apart then onto School C which is a further 17 miles. The trip back home is then another 28 miles. She can claim back 40p per mile for the trips between the schools but not her journey back home. Each mile she travels in her car costs her 14p. How much money will she have in total once her costs and claims have been accounted for?

c)   Johnny gets two buses to school each day, the first bus costs him £2.40 and the second is £1.90. He makes the journey 195 times a year, how much does this cost him in total?

d)   A teaching conference is to be held in Beijing. The outbound and return flight costs are shown in the table below. How much does Mrs Swift save by choosing to fly Option 1 in comparison to option 3.

Option 1	London	497.96	Doha	659.21	Beijing
Option 2	London	499	Abu Dhabi	729.49	Beijing
Option 3	London	499.98	Abu Dhabi	719.49	Beijing

e) The school party needs 121 cartons of orange juice, 56 bags of crisps, 16 loaves of bread and 12 bags of sweets. In total how much will this cost?

Item	Price
Cartons of Orange Juice (Pack of 11)	£2.99
Crips (Pack of 8)	£1.80
Bread (Per loaf)	£0.40
Sweets (Pack of 12)	£6.95

f) There are 124 children going on a school trip, the tickets cost £17.95 each. If the bill is greater than £2000, there is a 15% discount. How much is the total cost including the discount (if required)?

g) Mr Jennings performs a sponsored 1200-mile cycle over summer. Three teachers sponsor him, the details of which are below.

Miss Telford "50p per mile for the first 1000 miles, then 75p for each mile after."

Mr Hawkins "60p per mile."

Dr Granger "£1.20 per mile for the first 500, £1.00 per mile for the next 500 and 50p per mile for the next 200."

Work out the total amount of money raised.

8.3   I can perform division using a calculator

Explanation Example

Lucy must decide at the start of the year whether to buy daily, monthly or yearly bus tickets.

	Cost per ticket (£)	Has to buy	Total cost
Daily	2	195	390
Month	35	11	385
Yearly	400	1	400

Work out the cost per day, assuming she uses the bus 195 days per year and establish which ticket works out the best value for money?

From the table we can see that daily tickets cost **£2 per day**.

Second, monthly tickets

1. We need to calculate the cost per year

$$£35 \times 11 = £385$$

2. Then we need to divide by the number of days to find the cost per day.

$$£385 \div 195 = £1.97 \text{ per day}$$

Thirdly, yearly tickets

We know the tickets cost £400 per year. So to find the cost per day we need to divide £400 by the number of days.

$$£400 \div 195 = £2.05 \text{ per day}$$

From this we can see that the **monthly** tickets are the cheapest.

3.4   I can perform division using a calculator – TEST questions

a) Thirty Mereside School pupils went on a hiking trip. The total cost was £188.50. The bus cost £100 and the rest was spent on lunches. How much did each lunch cost?

b) Mrs Cauldy, the caretaker, travels a total of 50.75 miles in a week. This is made up of journeys to and from school, which is 3.625 miles away from her home. How many times did she perform the return journey that week?

c) The annual electricity bill for a school is £179400. This is based on lights and appliances being used for 8 hours per day, 195 days a year. How much does 1 hour of electricity cost the school on average?

d) Use the table below to work out who earned the most stars per day?

	Days at School	Stars Earned
Alfie	195	92
Beatrice	172	87
Calum	190	83
Della	192	90
Emily	189	46
Fran	180	86

e) If there are 39 weeks in a school year and 195 teaching days, what is the average number of teaching days per teaching week?

f) Seven boys and eight girls each order a new PE kit, consisting of a shirt and shorts. The total bill is £225. The shirts cost £9 each, how much do the shorts cost?

g) In total, the 402 pupils at Clifford Primary used 8522.4m^2 of paper in one year. Assuming they all used the same amount, how much did one pupil use?

8.5   I can perform compound conversions

Explanation Example

A car with a flat tyre is travelling at 98.4 meters per minute. You may assume 1 mile is 1610 meters. What is the speed of the car in miles per hour? Give your answer to two decimal places.

First let's convert meters into miles.

To do this we need to divide the number of meters we have, by how many meters go into a mile, in this case 1610.

(Tip: to check you are doing it correctly you can use your knowledge that a mile is larger than a meter. So when converting from meters to miles your answer needs to be getting smaller)

$$98.4 \div 1610 = 0.06111801242 \text{ miles per minute}$$

Next we need to convert from minutes to hours. To do this we need to multiply by 60.

(Tip: To check you are doing it correctly, remember you will travel a greater distance in an hour than in a minute, so your answer needs to be getting bigger.)

$$0.061 \times 60 = 3.6671 \text{ miles per hour}$$

Finally, we need to round to 2 decimal places.

(Tip: Remember to only round on the last step, rounding early can give a different answer)

This gives an answer of **3.67 mph**.

8.6   I can perform compound conversions - TEST questions

To revise conversions please see the conversion method on **page 66**.

a) Fuel was purchased at a cost of 1.20€ per litre. Knowing that 4.546 litres = 1 gallon and that £1 = 1.30€, how much is the cost in £ per gallon. Give your answer to the nearest penny.

b) Bryony completes the LRO Marathon in the USA. She averages a speed of 9 miles per hour. Using 1 mile = 8/5 km and 1 minute = 1/60 hour work out her time in km per minute.

c) A car is travelling at 13.4m/s. What is this in miles per hour? You may assume 1 mile is 1610 metres. Give your answer to two decimals places.

d) The bamboo plant in Dr Klein's garden is a type that under the optimum conditions can grow up to 40m a year. Assuming one day is precisely 24 hours, calculate the rate of growth in mm per hour. Give your answer to 2 decimal places. (Use 1 year as exactly 365 days)

e) A sponsored cycle across Spain covers a distance of 500km. Each km was sponsored at 1€ per km. 5M = 8KM. 1€ = £0.75. The total amount raised was £575. What was the sponsorship rate in €s per mile? Give your answer to the nearest whole cent.

f) Mrs Barrington has a textbook in which the density of gold is given as 0.698 pounds per cubic inch. Taking one cubic inch as 16.39 cubic centimetre and 1 pound as 453.59 grams, convert the density of gold into grams per cubic centimetre, giving your answer to one decimal place.

g) A trip around Spain covers a distance of 790km. The fuel for this trip cost 1.30€ per litre. Knowing that 4.546 litres = 1 gallon and that £1 is 1.05€, how much is the cost of the fuel in pounds per gallon.

9. Averages

Introduction

Averages is the all-encompassing term which describes not only the mean (add them all up, divide by how many there are) but also the mode (most common), the median (the one in the middle) and sometimes the range (difference between largest and smallest value). The questions referring to averages in the skills test use tables or graphs to represent the data.

9.1 Calculating Mean, Mode, Median and Range

Explanation Example

On a school sports day 16 girls throw a shot, the distances are recorded to the nearest metre and displayed in the table below.

Distance (m)	Frequency (F)
1	2
2	3
3	7
4	4

Example 1: How to calculate the mean

Calculate the **mean** distance of the shots thrown to the nearest cm?

When in a frequency table we need to multiply the frequency by the units, in this case distance thrown. The table below shows that 2 people threw the shot put 1 m, 3 threw the shot put 2 m and so on.

We then add up the total distance thrown by all students, then divide by the number of students.

Distance (m)	Frequency (F)	D × F
1	2	1 × 2 = 2
2	3	2 × 3 = 6
3	7	3 × 7 = 21
4	4	4 × 4 = 16
		Sum = 45

Mean = 45 ÷ 16 = **2.81m**

Example 2: How to calculate the median

On a schools sports day 16 girls throw a shot, the distance is recorded to the nearest m. Workout the median distance the shot was thrown to the nearest cm?

Median – the one in the middle.

Using the rule:

$$Put\ the\ set\ in\ ascending\ order\ then\ find\ the\ \frac{n+1}{2}^{th}\ term$$

Median = (16 + 1) ÷ 2 = **8.5th distance**

Distance (m)	Frequency (F)	Running total number of people
1	2	2
2	3	+ 5
3	7	←8.5 distance + 12
4	4	+ 16

Median distance = **3m**

Example 3: How to find the mode and range

On a school sports day 16 girls throw a shot, the distance is recorded to the nearest m. Workout the mode and range of the distances to the nearest cm?

Mode – the one that appears the most.
Range – maximum value subtract the minimum.

Distance (D)	Frequency (F)
1	2
2	3
3	7
4	4

Mode = **3m**
(7 people achieved this)

Range = 4m – 1m = **3m**

9.2   I can work out the mean, median, mode and range – SKILLS questions.

Work out the mean, median, mode and range of each of the following:

a) 2, 4, 4, 1, 4

b) 6, 5, 4, 6, 6

c) 5, 4, 2, 1, 7, 7

d) 10, 12, 7, 6, 85, 21

e) 23, 53, 19, 17, 11, 103

f) 46, 43, 2, 6

g) 18, 47, 41, 14, 5, 29, 44

h) 0, 1, 1, 0, 1, 0, 1

i) 2.1, 3.1, 4.2, 3.2, 3.3

j) 0.8, 0.3, 0, 0.5

k) 0.1, 0.3, 0.6, 0, 0.9

l) 0.5, 0.8, 0.7, 0.5, 0.8, 0.7, 0.5

For each of the following frequency tables work out the mean, median, mode and range:

m)

Amount (£)	Frequency
0.50	1
1.00	2
1.50	3
2.00	2
2.50	1

n)

Amount (£)	Frequency
5.00	4
10.00	4
15.00	6
20.00	3
25.00	2

o)

Amount (£)	Frequency
1.00	7
2.00	11
3.00	15
4.00	16
5.00	14

P)

Sweets	Frequency
1	6
2	4
3	5
4	1
5	7

9.3 I can work out the mean, median, mode and range – TEST questions

a) A teacher recorded the volume of water drank by each of her pupils, as shown in the table below.

Girls		Boys	
Water Drank (ml)	Number of Pupils	Water Drank (ml)	Number of Pupils
400	5	400	6
500	5	500	10
600	7	600	6
700	5	700	2
800	2	800	7

Select all **TRUE** statements from the list below:

i) The mean volume drank by the girls was more than the boys.

ii) More boys than girls drank 700ml of water or more.

iii) Twice as many girls than boys drank 400ml.

iv) There are more boys than girls.

v) The median girl drank 600ml of water.

vi) The median boy drank 600ml of water.

vii) One third of the pupils who drank 500ml were girls.

viii) The mode value drank by girls and boys was 500ml.

ix) One eighth of the pupils who drank 800ml were girls.

x) The range of water drank for both sets of pupils is 400ml.

xi) There are at least 20% more boys than girls.

xii) The mean amount drank by girls is 575ml.

b) A teacher summarised the 90 science test grades of his pupils, as shown in the table below (each of the 30 pupils took three tests).

GCSE Grade	Biology	Chemistry	Physics
9	1	4	0
8	1	3	2
7	5	4	3
6	7	4	9
5	4	5	6
4	3	4	4
3	3	3	4
2	4	2	2
1	2	1	0

Select all **TRUE** statements from the list below:

i) The range of grades for all three papers is the same.

ii) Chemistry has the highest mean grade of the three papers.

iii) The median grade for biology is 5.

iv) The lowest grade achieved in physics is Grade 1.

v) The mean grade for biology is less than 5.

vi) The median grade for physics is 5.

vii) Of the 90 grades achieved across the three papers, 1/6 were for grade 3.

viii) The median grade for chemistry is 5.

ix) Over 1/3 of pupils achieved a grade 7 or higher in chemistry.

x) The modal grade for biology is grade 6.

xi) The mean grade for physics is 5.2

xii) One sixth of the biology grades are Grade 7.

:) A head teacher summarised the heights of her 240 pupils. This is shown in the table below. The mean can be estimated by summing the *frequency × midpoint* column and dividing by the total number of pupils.

Heights (x)	Frequency (F)	Midpoint (cm)(M)	F × M
$120 \leq x < 130$	46	125	5750
$130 \leq x < 140$	47	135	6345
$140 \leq x < 150$	48	145	6960
$150 \leq x < 160$	49	155	7595
$160 \leq x < 170$	50	165	8250

Select all **TRUE** statements from the list below:

i)   The pupil with the median height is in the group $140 \leq x < 150$.

ii)   The estimated mean is 145.41cm.

iii) The estimated mean is 151.97cm.

iv)   At least 50% of the pupils are shorter than 150cm.

v)   The modal height can be estimated to be 165cm.

vi)   Increasing the group $120 \leq x < 130$ by 30% would take the number of pupils to 58.

vii) 60% of the pupils are 140cm or taller.

viii) The range of heights is 40cm.

ix)   The range of heights is 50cm.

x)   There are 230 pupils in total.

xi)   If the number of boys to girls is in a ratio 1:1, there are 120 girls.

xii) The largest section on a pie chart would represent 160 - 170cm.

9.4   Potential values

Potential values is a subtopic of averages. These questions are usually quite tricky and therefore it is good to get plenty of practice. They require you to determine certain facts based on your knowledge of averages and the data presented. We recommend that you become confident with the types of averages and their definitions, which can be revised on **page 101**, before continuing.

Explanation Example

A summary table of French test marks for Class A and Class B is displayed in the table below.

Class	Median	Mode	Range
A	73	65	21
B	69	62	33

We know certain facts about averages, for instance all values must be within the range. We know some values (in this instance the median and mode) and using these we can estimate the limits of the rest of the data.

a) At least one person scored 90 in test A, True or False?

We need to use the lowest mark we know someone achieved in test A, this would be the mode mark 65. We also know the range of marks. From this we can draw the following diagram.

Write out values you know – median and mode.

Adding the range of marks to the lowest mark gives us the highest possible mark. And subtracting the range from the highest mark gives us the lowest possible mark given the information we have.

From this we can see the highest possible mark is 86, and the lowest possible mark is 52. We can therefore say this statement is **FALSE**. It is not possible for anybody to have scored 90.

b) The lowest mark achieved in Class B was 32, True or False?

We can see that the highest mark we know of is the median which is 69. We know the range of marks is 33. From this we can draw the following diagram.

69 - 33 = 36   Range - 33
Min   ⌐ 62   69 ⌐
B   L   L   Max
                                    62 + 33 = 95

Subtracting the range from the highest mark we know gives us the lowest possible mark given the information we have.

$$69 - 33 = 36$$

Thus, the statement is **FALSE**; the lowest mark in class B was 36.

9.5 I can work out potential values using a summary table – TEST questions

a) The head of history at Malcolm-Grange summarised the scores the four Year 10 classes got in their tests.

	Marks (Percentage)		
Class	Median	Mode	Range
History A	65	60	32
History B	51	55	49
History C	80	79	5
History D	43	45	16

Select all **TRUE** statements from the list below:

i) From the four classes, the highest possible score anyone achieved was 100%.

ii) All pupils in history C achieved at least 70%.

iii) No one in history A could have scored less than 35.

iv) At least one pupil in history D achieved a score of 45.

v) All pupils in history C achieved at least 75%.

vi) At least one pupil in history B, could have achieved a score of 52.

vii) In class D over half the pupils achieved a score of 50% or more.

viii) The class with the smallest range had the highest median.

ix) The lowest possible mark anyone achieved was 6.

x) Everyone in history C scored less than 80%.

xi) Across the four classes at least half of the pupils achieved 50%.

xii) The most common score in history A was 65.

b) A council recorded the attendance rates of the three primary schools.

School	Attendance (Percentage)			
	Mean	Median	Mode	Range
Almgate	90	91	91	12
Bullroad	94	85	90	14
Carmington	82	91	85	23

Select all **TRUE** statements from the list below:

i) All of Almgate's students had an attendance above 88%.

ii) At least one pupil at Bullroad had an attendance of 75%.

iii) The most common attendance at Almgate was 91%.

iv) The highest attendance achieved at Almgate was 102%.

v) The highest attendance achieved at Bullroad was 99%.

vi) More than 50% of all pupils had attendance over 90%.

vii) One in two pupils at Almgate has attendance less than 90%.

viii) It is possible for at least one pupil in Carmington to have an attendance of 68%.

ix) The most common (in terms of attendance) at Bullroad was absent for every 1 in 10 days.

x) The mean at Almgate is the lowest possible attendance.

xi) No pupils as Bullroad had an attendance of less than 80%.

xii) No pupil at Carmington had an attendance less than 65%.

c) Westhorn Hill School organised a general knowledge quiz for its pupils and then summarised their scores by the three house groups: Black, Green and Orange.

	Score		
	Black	Green	Orange
Mean	70	47	59
Median	74	61	45
Mode	74	52	53
Range	23	37	15

Select all **TRUE** statements from the list below:

i)   The median was greater than the mean for all three house groups.

ii)   The maximum score anyone could have achieved was 93.

iii)   No one in Green house scored more than 84.

iv)   The most common score for Black house was 70.

v)   No one in Green scored fewer marks than 52.

vi)   In Orange house, 50% of people scored 45 or fewer.

vii)   The range of Green house scores is at least twice that of Orange's.

viii)   The lowest score for Orange house was greater than 40.

ix)   The lowest score for Black house was at least 51.

x)   The lowest score anyone could have potentially achieved was 19.

xi)   In Green house at least half of the class scored more than 60.

xii)   The mode and median were identical in Black house.

10. Data Representation

There are many ways in which data can be presented from box plots to two way tables. It is important that you practise each different question type and get used to interpreting the data that is provided. You need to learn what each chart and graph shows and what information you can derive from it. These questions make up a significant proportion of the written data section so please spend the time reading through the examples and method notes.

10.1   I can make inferences using a box plot

Introduction

Box plots are a simple way of representing the median, range and the quartiles of a data set. They are sometimes shown in pairs so that you can easily compare one data set to another.

Explanation Example

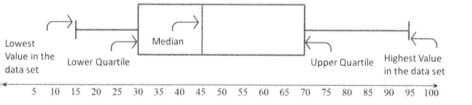

The **median** is the data value in the middle, the person 50% of the way through the sample, the one halfway through. There are two quartiles, first is 25% (1/4) of the way through the data which is called the **lower quartile** and then 75% (3/4) of the way through, which is called the **upper quartile**. All three can be seen in the diagram above.

Calculating the range:

The range can be calculated by doing the following:

Highest value in the data set – Lowest value in the data set

Calculating the interquartile range:

The interquartile range can be calculated by doing the following:

Upper Quartile – Lower Quartile

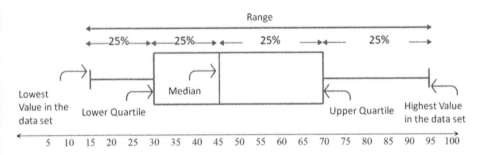

Using the box plot above shows the test scores of 100 students, use this to answer the following example questions:

Example 1: Calculate the median

From the diagram we can see the median is 45 Marks

Example 2: Find the number of students who achieved over 70 marks.

Form the diagram we can see that each section represents 25% of the students.

We can also see that 70 marks lies on the upper quartile, which means that 25% of the students achieved over this score. There are 80 students in total, so 25% of the students equals 20.

Therefore the answer is **20 Students**

Example 3 and 4: The box plots below show people's scores in music and drama tests.

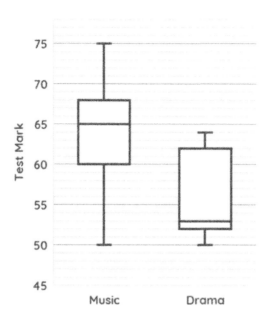

Test Question: Calculate the interquartile range of music marks.

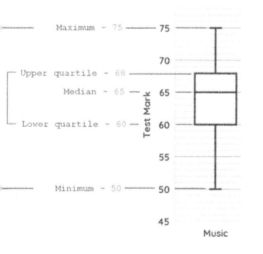

Looking at the box plot for music we can identify all the key features.

We can see the upper quartile is 68 marks and the lower quartile is 60 marks.

We can calculate the interquartile range with the following:

68 – 60 = 8 marks

Test Question: Calculate the range of drama marks.

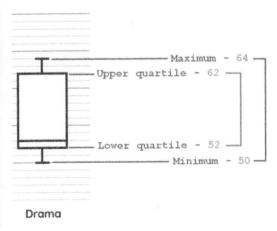

Drama

Looking at the box plot for drama we can identify all the key features.

We can see the highest mark is 64 and the lowest mark is 50.

We can calculate the range with the following:

$$64 - 50 = 14 \text{ marks}$$

10.2   I can make inferences using a box plot – TEST questions

a) A comparison of absence for Years 4 and 5 is conducted using the box plots below.

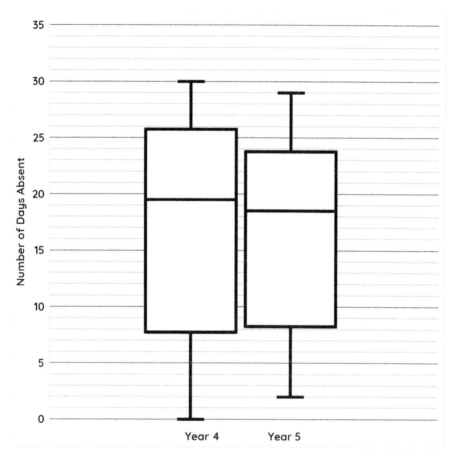

Select all **FALSE** statements from the list below:

i)   No one in Year 5 had 0 days absent.

ii)   The median for Year 4 is 19.5 days.

iii) The range of days for Year 4 is greater than that of Year 5.

iv)   The maximum number of days absent was 26.

v)   At least one pupil had no days absent.

vi)   In Year 5, the maximum number of days absent was 29.

vii)   Over 50% of Year 4 had at least 20 days absent.

viii)   The interquartile range is larger in Year 4 than Year 5.

ix)   Someone was absent for 32 days.

x)   In Year 5, the minimum number of days absent was 2.

xi)   In Year 4, at least one person had 30 days absent.

xii)   The median number of days is greater in Year 4 than Year 5.

b) Mr Peek compares the Mathematics test results of Class A to Class B

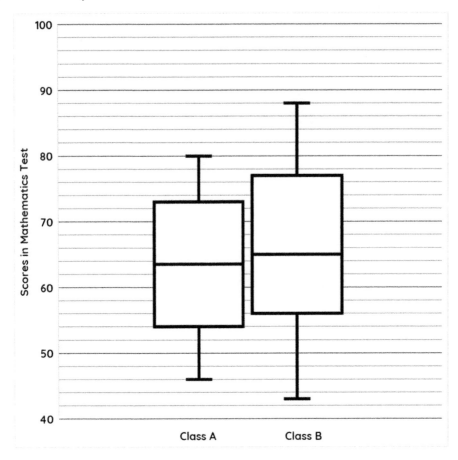

Select all **FALSE** statements from the list below:

i) The upper quartile for Class A is 73.

ii) Class B has a larger range of scores than Class A.

iii) The lower quartile for Class A is 59.

iv) The highest mark scored was from Class A.

v) The median score of Class B is 65.

vi) The median score of Class A is 64.

vii) The range of marks for Class A is 34.

viii) Over 50% of Class B scored less than 56 marks.

ix) The upper quartile for Class B is 77.

x) The interquartile range of Class A is 31.

xi) At least one person scored 88.

xii) More people in Class B achieved a higher mark than those in Class A.

c) The Head of Key Stage four produces the following box plots to compare absence rates in Year 10 and Year 11.

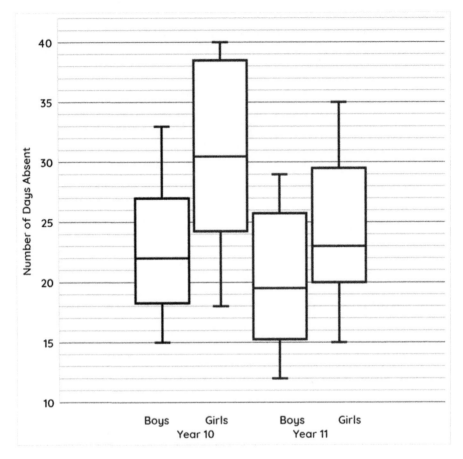

Select all **TRUE** statements from the list below:

i)   The individual with the fewest days absent was a Year 10 boy.

ii)   The median number of days absent for Year 11 girls was 22.

iii)   The range of Year 10 girls was greater than Year 10 boys.

iv)   The range of Year 11 boys' days absent is 17.

v)   Precisely fifty percent of Year 10 boys had 25 days absent or fewer.

vi)   One student has 13 days absent.

vii)   The interquartile range is smaller for Year 10 boys compared to

Year 11 boys.

viii)   A Year 10 girl had the most days absent.

ix)   At least one student had 40 days absent.

x)   The interquartile is the smallest for Year 10 girls.

xi)   Year 11 boys is the group with most days absent.

xii)   The median number of days absent for Year 10 boys was 29.

10.3   I can make inferences using a scatter graph

Introduction

Scatter graphs are a way of representing two bits of data relating to one item or person. For example, one person's scores in two exams, or one car's distance travelled and the amount of petrol used. Take a look at the example scatter graph below:

Explanation Example

The graph below shows three people's scores in an English and Mathematics test.

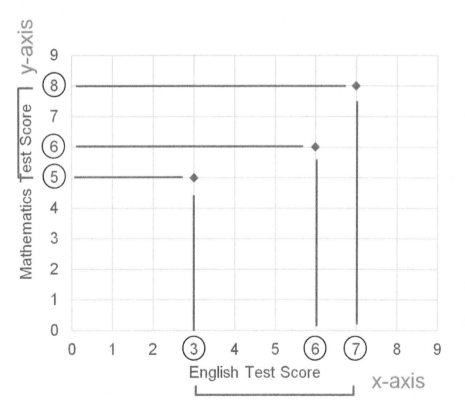

What this graph shows:

This graph shows three students

- Student 1: 7 in English, 8 in maths
- Student 2: 6 in English, 6 in maths
- Student 3: 3 in English, 5 in maths

Calculating the range:

To calculate the range we subtract the lowest score from the highest:

- Range of maths scores 8 − 5 = 3
- Range of English scores 7 − 3 = 4

Calculating the mean:

We need to add up the scores then divide by how many there are.

- Mean maths = (8 + 6 + 5) ÷ 3 = 6.33
- Mean English = (7 + 6 + 3) ÷ 3 = 5.33

Finding the median

We need to find the middle value:

- 6 is the Median maths score
- 6 is the Median English score

Example Test Question 1: At least one student scored an 8 in the mathematics test, True or False?

We can see that student 1 scored a 7 in English and 8 in maths. Thus this statement is **TRUE**.

Example Test Question 2: Two students scored a level 6 in the English test, True or False?

We can see the English scores are 3, 6, and 7. Therefore this statement is **FALSE**.

a) Below the results of a maths and English test are displayed for students of one specific class.

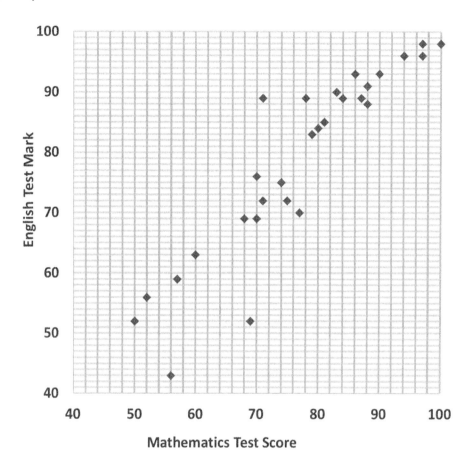

Select all **TRUE** statements from the list below:

i)   The lowest mark in the English test was 43.

ii)   Forty people took both tests.

iii)   More people scored a higher mark in English than in maths.

iv)   The person who scored 56 in mathematics scored 44 in English.

v)   The highest English mark was 98.

vi)   Two pupils scored 98 in English.

vii) One person scored 89 in English.

viii) The person that achieved a mark of 50 in mathematics also achieved a mark of 50 in English.

ix) The highest mark in mathematics was 98.

x) A person who achieved 70 in English would be expected to achieve 70 in mathematics

xi) Ten people scored less than 70 in mathematics.

xii) One person scored the same in English and mathematics.

) A school offers French revision lessons before registration to see if this helps o improve test marks. Below shows the marks in a French test and school ourney time for a group of students. Longer journey times generally resulted n less time in the French revision class.

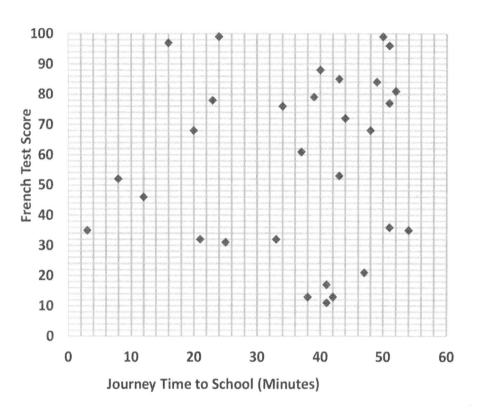

Journey Time to School (Minutes)

Select all **TRUE** statements from the list below:

i)   No journey to school took longer than 60 minutes.

ii) Only three people scored less than 20 marks in the French test.

iii) The pupil who took 54 minutes to get to school achieved fewer than 40 marks in the French test.

iv) No one who took more than 30 minutes to get to school achieved a mark above 50.

v)   At least one pupil achieved 99 on their French test.

vi) The range of journey times was 51 minutes.

vii) Seven people scored less than 10 marks in the French test.

viii) The median journey time to school was 30 minutes.

ix) The range in French Test marks was 90.

x) Brian achieved a mark of 35, which means his journey to school was 3 minutes.

xi) No journey to school was shorter than 5 minutes.

xii) Five people scored between 70 and 80 in the French test.

c) The chart below displays information about the distance student's travel to school and the associated cost of this travel.

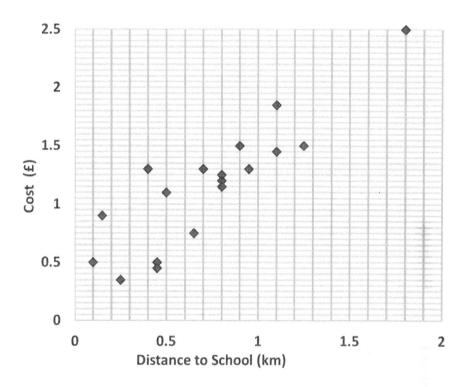

Select all **FALSE** statements from the list below:

i)   One person travelled over 1.9km to school.

ii)   No one travelled less than 200 metres to school.

iii) The graph shows 19 people in total.

iv)   Only one person's journey to school cost £1.50.

v)   The range of costs is £2.15.

vi)   At least six people lived within half a kilometre of the school.

vii) A random pupil's journey costs £1.20; this means their journey was 0.8km.

viii) In total, over £50 was spent on their journey to school.

ix) The most expensive journey cost £2.60.

x) The furthest journey was 1.8km.

xi) Two people's journey cost 50p.

xii) One person travelled exactly 1km to school.

0.5   I can make inferences using a line graph

Introduction

Line graphs are similar to scatter plots in their lay out but the points on the graph are joined up. They are commonly used to show how something changes over time. The idea being you have points that you join up with a line which shows you the general trend of the data and also enables you to estimate values between the data points by using the line.

Explanation Example

The graph below shows the temperature of two locations in a school over the spring term.

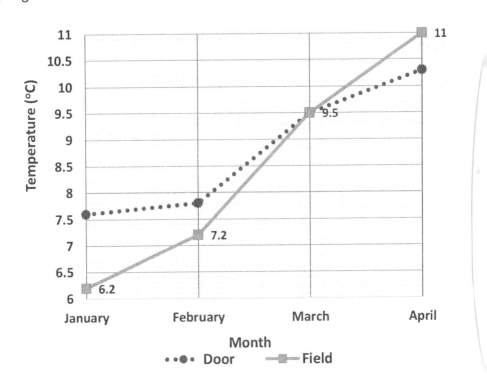

Find the range of temperatures:

To calculate the range we subtract the lowest temperature from the highest:

- Door Temp. range = 10.3 − 7.6 = 2.7
- Field Temp. range = 11 − 6.2 = 4.8

Calculating the mean:

We need to add up the temperatures then divide by the number of readings:

- Door mean = (10.3 + 9.5 +7.8 +7.6) ÷ 4 = 8.8
- Field mean = (11 + 9.5 +7.2 + 6.2) ÷ 4 = 8.475

Example Question: Calculate the percentage temperature increase for the field from February to March. Give your answer to 2 decimal places.

To calculate percentage increase we need to use the equation (found in the help sheet)

$$Percentage\ increase\ = \left(\frac{Increase}{Original}\right) \times 100$$

Temperature in February = 7.2 °C

Temperature in March = 9.5 °C

Temperature increase = 9.5 - 7.2 = 2.3 °C

We can then insert these figures to the equation above, which gives:

$$\left(\frac{2.3}{7.2}\right) \times 100 = 31.944444 = 31.94$$

This the percentage increases as **31.94 %** *(2 d.p.)*

a) The average reading age of pupils at a school is compared to the regional average.

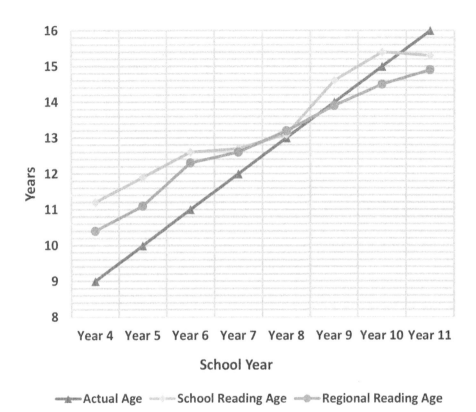

Select all **FALSE** statements from the list below:

i) The school average was greater than the actual age for all but one school year.

ii) There was less than one year between the school average and regional average for the Year 4.

iii) The range of reading ages for the region was 4 years.

iv) In total 8 school years are represented on the graph.

v) The school's Year 7's had an average reading age of 12.

vi) From Year 8 to Year 11, the region had a higher reading age than the school.

vii) The regional average reading age was more than one year below their actual age for Year 11.

viii) The actual age of Year 4's is 9.

ix) The median school reading age is 12.9.

x) The regional average reading age for Year 11 was 14.2.

xi) The median regional reading age is 12.9 years.

xii) The maximum school reading age was 15.1.

b) The temperatures at two locations throughout the year at Brookhill School are displayed below.

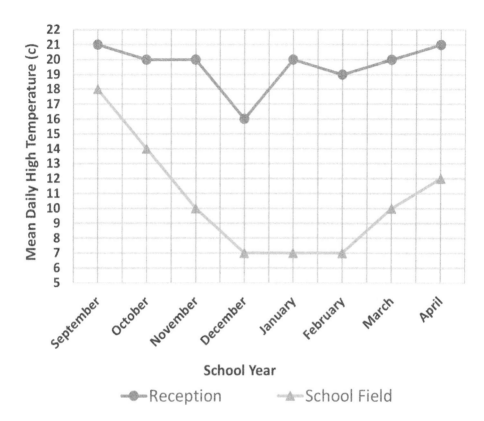

School Year

Select all **TRUE** statements from the list below

i) The school field was warmer than reception for 2 months.

ii) The maximum temperature was 21 degrees.

iii) The lowest reception temperature was in December.

iv) The range of temperatures on the school field was 10.

v) April was cooler than March in reception.

vi) January was colder than February on the field.

vii) The school field was 9 degrees in November.

viii) The school field was 20 degrees in April.

ix) In March, reception was 20 degrees.

x)   In March the field was 12 degrees.

xi) The median school field temperature was 12 degrees.

xii) The range of temperatures in reception was 5 degrees.

c) Emily and Jack were tested on their Spanish every month for an entire year. Their marks were recorded on the line chart shown below.

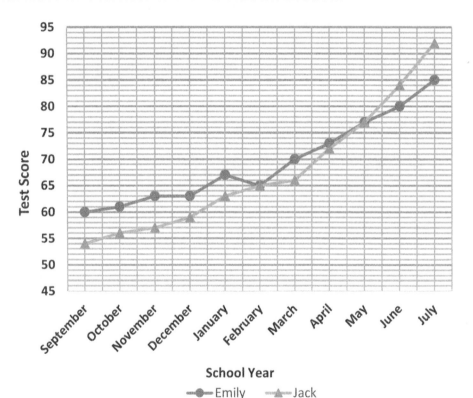

Select all **TRUE** statements from the list below

i)   Emily's test score in September was 60.

ii) The range of Jack's scores is 40.

iii) Emily and Jack achieved the same score in February.

iv) Jacks score was higher than Emily's for two months.

v)   Emily's score was higher in January than February.

vi)   Jack's median score was 60.

vii)   Emily's maximum score was 85.

viii)   Jack's score in July was 92.

ix)   The range of Emily's scores was 20.

x)   Jacks score increased every month.

xi)   Jack's lowest score was 47.

xii)   The range of Emily's scores was 22.

10.7 I can make inferences using a bar chart

Introduction

Bar charts are another way of viewing a single data set or comparing multiple data sets. They are amongst the simplest forms of representing data but there are a few variations that you need to familiarise yourself with. These are covered in the following examples.

Explanation Example

The graph below shows Year 3 pet ownership split into what the boys own and what the girls own. The person who summarised the data stacked the values of dog, cat and other pet ownership on top of each other. This is often how they appear in the actual exam questions.

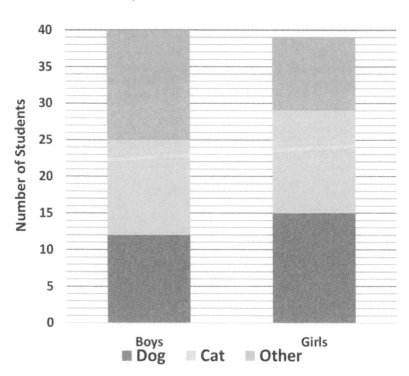

Example Question 1: Calculate how many boys had dogs, cats and others pets.

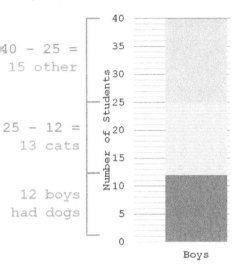

$40 - 25 =$
15 other

$25 - 12 =$
13 cats

12 boys
had dogs

By looking at the key we can see the top section shows others, middle section is cats, and the bottom section is dogs.

We then need to look at the height of each section independently to find out how many are in each section.

From this we can work out that the boys owned 12 dogs, 13 cats and 15 other pets.

Example Question 2: Calculate the percentage of girls who own dogs. Give your answer to 2 decimal places.

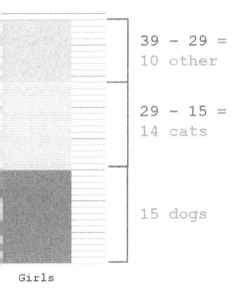

$39 - 29 =$
10 other

$29 - 15 =$
14 cats

15 dogs

First we have to calculate how many girls have each pet in the same way as the previous example. From this we can work out that the girls owned 15 dogs, 14 cats and 10 other pets.

Next we need to work out the percentage of dogs owned by girls compared to the total number of pets owned by girls.

To do this we calculate:

$$\left(\frac{15}{39}\right) \times 100 = 38.461..$$

$$= 38.46\%$$

10.8   I can make inferences using a bar chart – TEST questions

a) The graph below shows the year-on-year change of those who received the equivalent of 5 A*-C grade GCSEs at Sectorwold School.

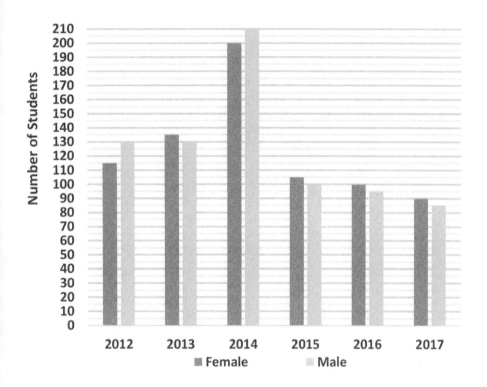

Select all **TRUE** statements from the list below

   i)   The year 2017 saw the lowest number of passes for both males and females.

   ii)   The number of females who passed increased between 2012 and 2013.

   iii)   The number of female passes increased by over 50% from 2013 to 2014.

   iv)   Only 85 males passed in 2017.

   v)   Across the six years the median number of boys who passed is 110.

vi) The number of female passes increases every year.

vii) 311 males passed in the years 2015, 2016 and 2017.

viii) Across the six years the median number of boys who passed is 124.

ix) The range of number passes each year for females is 110.

x) From 2016 to 2017 the number of passes dropped by 20%.

xi) The range of number passes each year for males is 115.

xii) Across the six years, 855 females passed.

b) The teachers at Rother Junior School asked the pupils in each year their preferred sport. The results are represented below in a stacked bar chart.

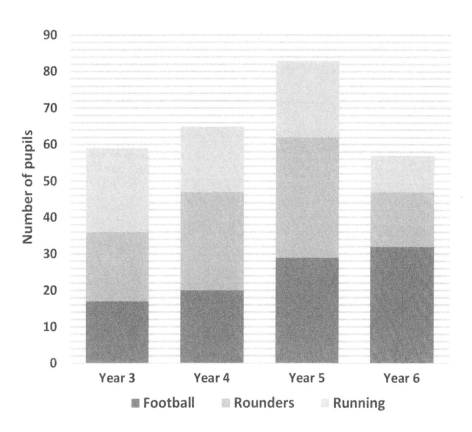

Select all **FALSE** statements from the list below

i) More Year 3s preferred running to rounders.

ii) The most popular sport in the school was rounders.

iii) More children in Year 4 preferred running to those in Year 5.

iv) The median number of children who preferred rounders is 23.

v) 21 Year 4s chose football as their favourite sport.

vi) The number who preferred running decreased with each school year.

vii) There are 60 children in Year 3.

viii) 18 children in Year 4 chose running as their favourite sport.

ix) There were 94 children in the school whose favourite sport was rounders.

x) In Year 4, over half of the children chose rounders.

xi) In Year 6, 10 children preferred running.

xii) There were 261 children in the whole school.

c) Mrs Wood at Torrington Girls Grammar produced the following graph of GCSE music grades for years 2014 to 2018.

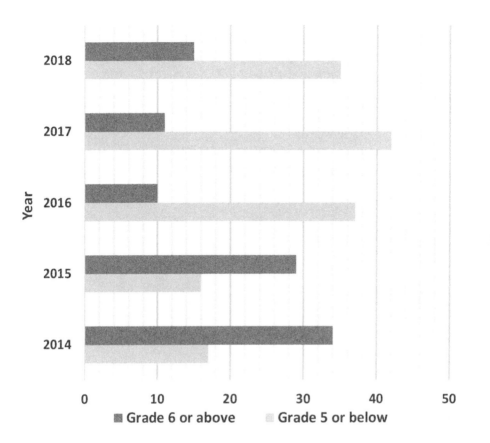

Select all **TRUE** statements from the list below

i)   There were 51 children taking their GCSE in 2014.

ii)   In 2016, 10 more people achieved grade 5 or below compared to 2014.

iii) The maximum number of grade 6 or above was achieved in 2014.

iv)   The number of pupils in 2016 was 47.

v)   Fewer people achieved grade 6 or above in 2018 than in 2017.

vi)   Across the five years 99 people achieved grade 6 or above.

vii) In 2015, two-thirds of people achieved a grade 5 or below.

viii) 2015 to 2016 saw the biggest percentage change in pupils achieving grade 6 or above.

ix) Over the five years, 223 people took GCSE music.

x) In 2018, 25% of the results were for grade 6 or above.

xi) One third of pupils in 2014 achieved a grade 5 or below.

xii) In 2017, 41 people achieved a grade 5 or below.

QTS LITERACY TUTOR
WWW.LITERACYSKILLSTEST.CO.UK

FREE ONLINE LITERACY SKILLS TEST
EXPERT 1 TO 1 TUITION WITH OUR QTS SPECIALISTS

--- **WHAT QTS LITERACY TUTOR HAS TO OFFER** ---

Spelling Practice

Punctuation Questions

Grammar Section

Comprehension Resources

Practice Tests

Expert Tutors

Correct Format

New Question Formats

Visit www.literacyskillstest.co.uk to take a Free Full Practice Test today.

10
LITERACY SKILLS TESTS

97%
LEARNER PASS RATE

490
TEST QUESTIONS

10.9   I can make inferences using a cumulative frequency graph

Cumulative frequency graphs show a running total which is plotted on the Y axis. In the numeracy skills test the cumulative frequency often represents the number of students in a given context. You can determine averages using these curves and make a number of inferences.

Explanation Example

The graph below shows the ICT Test Marks of 30 pupils.

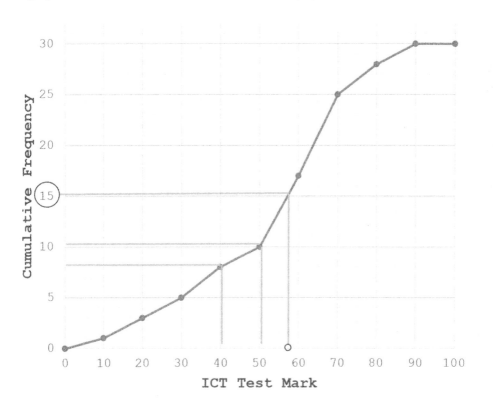

Question 1: How many people scored 50 marks or fewer?

Looking at the 50 mark on the x – axis we can go up the cumulative frequency line and look across at the y-axis and see that **10** people scored 50 or fewer on the test.

Question 2: How many people scored 40 marks or fewer?

Similarly, looking at the 40 mark, we see that 8 people scored 40 or fewer. We can use this information to work out that **2** people scored between 41 and 50.

Question 3: Calculate the range of marks

Looking between 90 and 100 we see the graph is flat indicating that no one scored between 91 and 100.

The range of scores is **90** (90 – 0).

Question 4: Calculate the median mark

To find the median we need to half the total number of people: 30 ÷ 2 = 15. The median is the 15th person's score. Therefore, going along from 15 to the curve then down to the x-axis we can estimate the median mark to be **57**.

Question 5: Find the upper and lower quartile

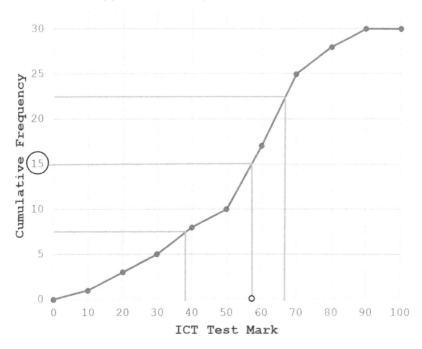

ICT Test Mark

To find the lower quartile we need to find ¼ of the total number of people. The lower quartile in this example is the 7.5th persons score, going along from there, to the line then down to the x-axis we can estimate the lower quartile mark as 38.

To find the upper quartile we need to find 3/4 of the total number of people. The upper quartile in this example is the 22.5th persons score; going along from there to the line then down to the x-axis we can estimate the upper quartile mark as 66.

Question 6: Find the inter-quartile range.

To find the inter-quartile range we subtract the lower quartile from the upper quartile.

66 – 38 = **28**

questions

a) The graph below shows the times taken for 38 people to complete a race.

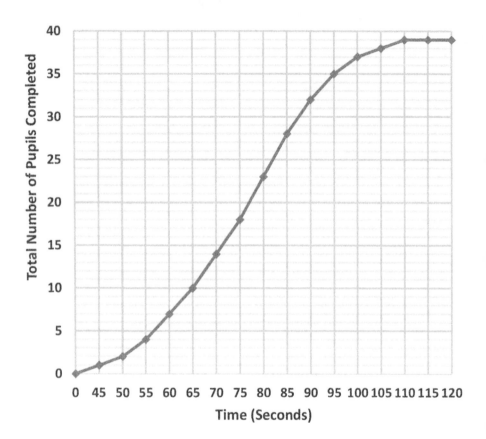

Select all **TRUE** statements from the list below:

i)   No pupils finished the race in under 45 seconds.

ii)   The slowest person finished in less than 110 seconds.

iii)   In total 40 people ran the race.

iv)   The median can be estimated at 60 seconds.

v)   The lower quartile is 50 seconds.

vi)   90 seconds for the upper quartile.

vii)   18 pupils finished in 75 seconds or less.

viii)   No pupils finished in the interval 55 to 60 seconds.

 ix)   Three pupils finished between 90 and 95 seconds.

b) The graph above shows the amount of time that a group of students spend revising.

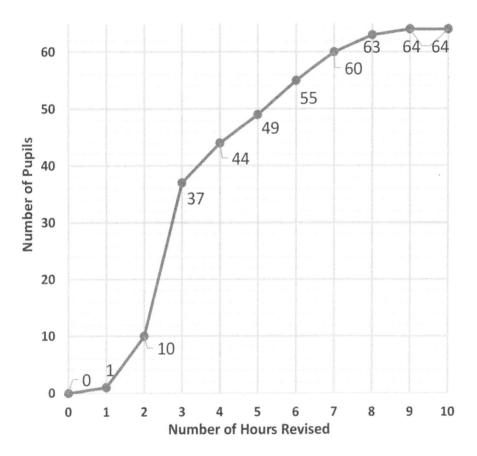

Select all **TRUE** statements from the list below:

  i)   There were 64 pupils in the group.

 ii)   No pupils revised more than 10 hours.

iii)   10 pupils revised for 2 hours or fewer.

iv)   18 pupils revised from 2 to 3 hours.

v)	No pupils revised for less than one hour.
vi)	No pupils revised for more than 9 hours.
vii)	The median can be estimated at 2 hours and 45 minutes.
viii)	The upper quartile suggests that 75% of people revised for under 4 hours.
ix)	Twice as many people revised between 5 and 6 hours than between 7 and 8 hours.

10.11 I can make inferences using a pie chart

Pie charts are a good way of presenting different proportions of data, as at a glance you can see the largest and smallest sections and compare these to another pie chart if required. It is important to note, two pie charts might represent different numbers of people/students etc but appears the same size and therefore may not be directly comparable at a glance.

Explanation Example

This pie chart shows the GCSE choices of 26 pupils

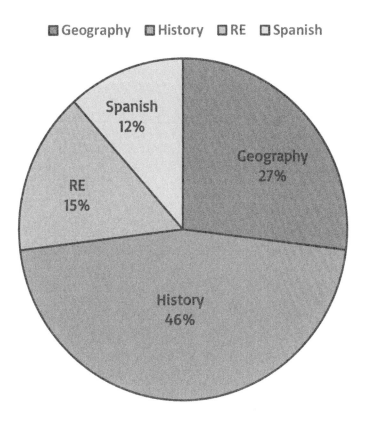

History is the most popular choice of subject with 46% of people choosing it; geography second; RE third and finally Spanish.

Example Question 1: Calculate how many students study each subject:

We can work out the amount of people studying each subject by calculating a percentage of an amount.

- History - **46% of 26** = 0.46 × 26 = 11.96 = 12 people
- Geography - **27% of 26** = 0.27 × 26 = 7.02 = 7 people
- RE - **15% of 26** = 0.15 × 26 = 3.9 = 4 people
- Spanish - **12% of 26** = 0.12 × 26 = 3.12 = 3 people

Example Test Question 1: Calculate the percentage point difference between geography and history.

This question refers to percentage points, rather than percentage change. This means we need to look at the percentages as numbers and find the difference between the numbers.

We can see that geography is 27% and history is 46%, so we must find the difference between these numbers.

$$46 - 27 = 19 \text{ percentage points}$$

Example Test Question 2: Find the fraction of students who studied RE, give your answer in its simplest for.

We know that 15% of students chose RE. 15% can also be written as $\frac{15}{100}$ (Remember percentages are out of 100)

Next, we need to simplify the fraction. We can do this by dividing the top and bottom by 5.

$$\frac{15}{100} = \frac{3}{20}$$

a) The pie charts below display a school's GCSE subject choices.

2014 has 62 GCSE students.

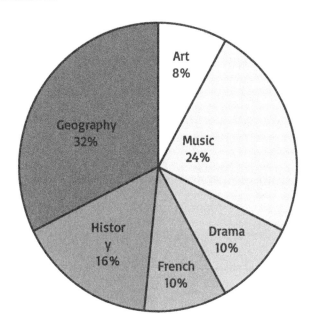

2015 has 81 GCSE students

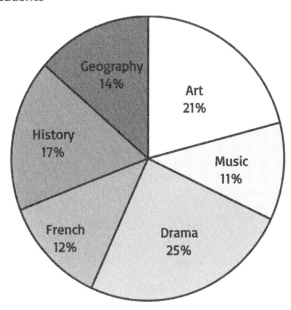

Select all **TRUE** statements from the list below:

i)   Twelve fewer people chose art in 2014 than in 2015.

ii) Drama was the most popular subject across both years.

iii) 3/7 of people in both years two chose art.

iv) In 2014, 8/25 people chose geography.

v)   Twice as many people in school A chose music than in school B.

vi) One tenth of people chose drama in school A.

vii) The number studying history increased by 40% from 2014 to 2015.

viii) The number studying art decreased by 40% from 2014 to 2015.

ix) One quarter of people chose drama in school B.

x)   Across both years 20 people studied French.

xi) Three times as many people studied drama in 2015 compared to 2014.

xii) geography was the least popular subject in 2015.

b) The university choices of 193 A level students are displayed below.

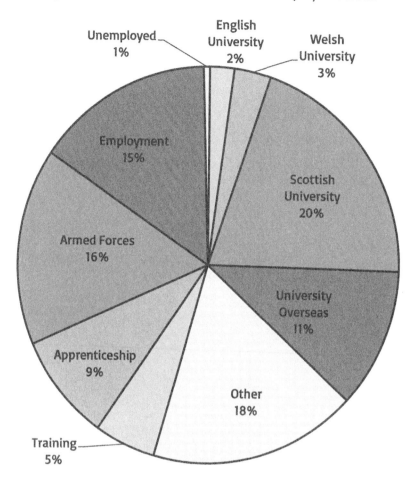

Select all **TRUE** statements from the list below:

i)   More people attended universities outside of Scotland than in Scotland.

ii) Three people became unemployed.

iii) Seventeen people went onto an apprenticeship.

iv) One fifth of students went to a Scottish university.

v)   Unemployment was the smallest destination.

vi) 9/50 of people went to Other destinations

vii) The most popular destination. was to attend a Scottish University.

viii) The range of number of people to each destination was from 1 to 39.

ix) 0.15 of people went in employment.

x) Eight times as many people joined the armed forces than went to an English University.

xi) Thirty-seven people were in other.

xii) 1/5 of people went into Training.

c) The GCSE ICT grades obtained by students at Airdale High School in 2016 and 2017 are compared using the pie charts below.

233 student's grades in 2016

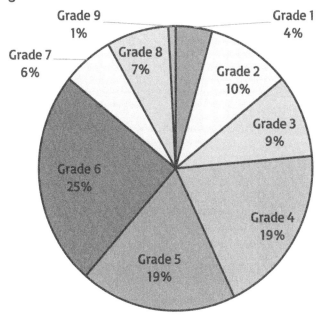

71 student's grades in 2017

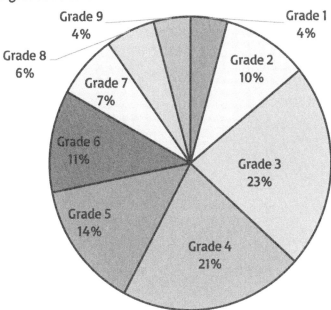

A strong pass is grades 5,6,7,8 and 9

Select all **TRUE** statements from the list below:

i) One hundred and thirty people achieved a strong pass in 2016.

ii) Grade 1 was the lowest percentage grade in 2017.

iii) More people achieved a grade 9 in 2016 than 2017.

iv) The number achieving a grade 1 in 2017 was a decrease of 80% from 2016.

v) There were four times fewer people taking GCSE ICT in 2017.

vi) Thirty people achieved a strong pass in 2017.

vii) Only one third of the number of people achieved a grade 4 in 2017 compared to 2016.

viii) The percentage of grade 3 increased by 100% from 2016 to 2017.

ix) Forty-four people achieved a grade 5 in 2016.

x) Eight people achieved a grade 8 or 9 in 2016.

xi) Grade 6 was the highest percentage grade in 2016.

xii) Sixteen people achieved a grade 3 in 2017.

10.13 I can make inferences using a two-way table

Introduction

Generally, one-way tables are just a way of showing the raw data. Two-way tables are a way of summarising data in number form. Like we saw in some of the graphs, we can have say test scores and then break this down by subject or by gender and easily compare the data presented.

Explanation Example

The table below shows the percentage of students who passed English, maths and science exams over a three year period for two separate schools.

Acorn School

Year	English (%)	Mathematics (%)	Science (%)
2015	75	74	73
2016	71	73	76
2017	72	73	79

Beech College

Year	English (%)	Mathematics (%)	Science (%)
2015	63	72	78
2016	68	65	73
2017	72	67	69

What these tables show:

In 2016, 76% passed science at Acorn School

In 2015, 63% passed English at Beech College.

Example Test Question 1: Calculate the percentage point difference between the numbers of people who passed mathematics at Acorn School in 2015 to 2017.

This question refers to percentage points, rather than percentage change. This means we need to look at the percentages as numbers and find the difference between the numbers.

We can see that mathematics in 2015 is 74% and mathematics in 2017 73%, so we must find the difference between these numbers.

$$74- 73 = 1 \text{ percentage point}$$

Example Test Question 2: In which year did Beech College have the greatest range of passes across all three subjects?

For this we need to work out the rank of pass percentages across all three years. This is the highest pass percentage – Lowest pass percentage.

2015: 78- 63 = 15

2016: 73- 65 = 8

2017: 72- 67 = 5

From this we can see the year with the greatest range is **2015**

a) The test results of 5 schools in the Yora Academy Trust are displayed in the table below.

	Average End of Year Test Percentage (%)				
English Faculty	Alfarm	Betrum	Calmwall	Dentons	Ebolt
Drama	71	93	64	42	51
English Language	73	87	53	63	61
English Literature	78	87	72	69	62
Mathematics Faculty					
ICT	84	66	79	72	60
Further Mathematics	80	53	50	58	42
Mathematics	82	72	64	63	62

Select all **FALSE** statements from the list below:

i) The English Faculty at Betrum outperformed the mathematics faculty in every subject.

ii) Across all five schools, ICT had the highest mean mark.

iii) Pupils at Denton studying drama had a higher average mark than at Ebolt.

iv) The ICT average score for Betrum was 10% higher than Ebolt.

v) Alfram had the highest range of scores across the 6 subjects.

vi) The lowest average score was for further mathematics at Ebolt.

vii) The mean English Language Score in the region was 73.6

viii) The mean English Language Score was higher than the mean English Literature score.

ix) The range of marks for the mathematics Faculty at Calmwall was 29.

x) For the entire region, the median drama score was 64.

xi) At Alfram all pupils taking Further mathematics scores less than 80%.

xii) The highest Average Percentage was for Betrum's drama pupils.

b) The results of a repeated test for pupils in English intervention at Chalington Grange are displayed in the table below.

	Dec	Jan	Feb	Mar	Apr	May
Amy	64	66	71	80	88	93
Bella	64	65	66	69	72	74
Charlie	75	72	71	68	63	60
David	50	60	42	66	64	67
Eric	41	48	63	65	64	68
Felicity	47	51	53	55	54	59

Select all **FALSE** statements from the list below:

i)   David and Eric have the same mean score across the 6 months.

ii)   January had the lowest range of scores of any month.

iii) Bella has the smallest range of scores.

iv)   Felicity's mean score was 82.

v)   Amy scored more than 80 in 1/3 of the months.

vi)   Charlie's score constantly increased.

vii) March and April have the same range of scores.

viii) Amy's mean score was 77.

ix)   February had a mean score of 52.

x)   The maximum score was 88.

xi)   In December, the median score was 57.

xii) The minimum score was 41.

c) The types of drinks preferred at Bromscedar Academies Trust displayed in the table below

Beverages	Groups of People			
	Primary	Secondary	Post 16	Staff
Cola	75	427	27	57
Hot Drinks	2	156	56	162
Juice	103	156	22	89
Lemonade	66	356	69	73
Water	46	177	56	124
Total	292	1272	230	505

Select all **TRUE** statements from the list below:

i)   Primary was the second largest group of people.

ii)   The least popular drink, across the four groups, was Juice.

iii)   For Staff, the most popular beverage was hot drinks.

iv)   The range between the groups of favourite beverages for Post 16 is 47.

v)   The mean group size for hot drinks is 94.

vi)   Across all groups of people and beverages, primary hot drinks had the fewest amount.

vii)   Including all four groups, cola was the most popular beverage.

viii)   Three times as many secondary school pupils preferred cola compared to primary school pupils.

ix)   One in five staff listed cola as their favourite drink.

x)   The mean group size for Lemonade is 100.

xi)   In total, 3742 people were surveyed.

xii)   Primary drank the highest percentage of Juice per group.

11. Other Data interpretation questions

The numeracy skills test contains a few very unique topics which you may never have encountered before. In this section you will see explanations of these topics and examples to help you understand how to answer these questions in your actual exam.

11.1   I can work with formulas and weighting Introduction

There are a number of formulae that appear in the numeracy skills test. These are given to you at the start of a question and you then have to use the data provided and substitute values into the formula in order to calculate the correct answer.

Explanation Example

The final mark for an English qualification is based on the formula shown below. Use this and the table to answer the following questions.

$$\text{Final mark} = \frac{(Oral) + (2 \times Reading) + (3 \times Writing)}{6}$$

Student	Oral	Reading	Writing
J	75	73	68
K	58	61	83

Example 1: Calculate the final mark for student J

By substituting the text for the relevant values, we can obtain values for the final mark.

$$\frac{(75) + (2 \times 73) + (3 \times 68)}{6} = \frac{425}{6} = 70.83$$

Student J final mark = **70.83**

Example 2: Calculate the final mark for student k

By substituting the text for the relevant values, we can obtain values for the final mark.

$$\frac{(58) + (2 \times 61) + (3 \times 83)}{6} = \frac{429}{6} = 71.5$$

Student **K** final Mark = **71.5**

Thus we can see that student K achieved the highest mark.

1.2   I can work with formulas and weighting – TEST questions

a) The final marks for an English qualification are given using the following formula:

$$Final\ mark = (0.8 \times Test\ 1\ mark) + (0.2 \times Test\ 2\ mark)$$

The results of three students are shown below.

	Test 1	Test 2
Amber	64	52
Ben	63	64
Charlie	56	93

Work out who achieved the highest final mark using the formula.

b) Mrs Haltby needs to convert 203 degrees Fahrenheit to Celsius. She is told that to obtain the temperature in Celsius she must:

Take 32 away from the Fahrenheit temperature.

Then, times the answer by 5.

Then, divide this answer by 9.

Work out the temperature in Celsius.

c) Using the following area for a triangle work out how much bigger than 15cm² a triangle of height 17cm, width 23cm is.

$$Area\ of\ triangle = \tfrac{1}{2} \times height \times width$$

d) The one hundred and one pupils in Year 3 at Corkridge Primary were asked how many siblings they each have. The data collected is displayed in the table below.

No. of siblings (S)	Frequency (F)	S × F
1	47	47
2	24	48
3	16	
4	14	
Sum	101	

The mean number of siblings can be calculated by dividing the sum of the S × F column by the number of pupils.

Complete the table and calculate the mean number of siblings, rounding your answer to two decimal places.

e) The formula for working out the final mark for the French GCSE is given by:

$$\frac{(2 \times \textit{Writing Test Mark}) + \textit{Oral Test Mark} + \textit{Listening Test Mark}}{4}$$

Using the scores of Sharon and Tanya given below work out the highest mark.

	Writing	Oral	Listening
Sharon	78	75	73
Tanya	74	79	83

f)   The volume of a sphere can be calculated using the formula,

$$\frac{4}{3} \times 3.14 \times r \times r \times r$$

where r is the radius.

If the radius of a spherical desk globe is 4cm, work out its volume to the nearest 3 decimal places.

g)   Wilkinson's Academy Year 9s are going on a trip to the Eureka! National Children's Museum in Halifax. It took 30 minutes to complete the journey.

Journey	Miles
Wilkinson's to M62	2
M62 to A629	6
A629 to A6193	12.8
A6193 to Eureka!	2.1

The average speed can be calculated by the dividing the distance in miles divided by the time taken. Work out the average speed, in miles per hour, from the school to Eureka!

h) A school is calculating the cost of borrowing £10,000 in order to fund a revamp of its sports facilities. The interest the charity charges is 2% per year. The school intends to pay back the loan in one year.

The total amount the school has to pay back can be calculated using the formula below.

$$Total\ cost = A\ (£) \times (1 + P)$$

A = Amount borrowed

P = Percentage interest as a decimal

How much will the school have to pay back at the end of the year?

11.3 I can work out the best price when considering discounts and offers

Introduction

These questions appear in tables and you have to use the data to perform multi-step calculations which often require a comparison of prices or discounts.

Explanation Example

Greenhill Academy needs to buy 115 tables for classrooms in the new Sixth Form building. The two approved suppliers both have offers available as shown in the table.

Shop	Cost (£)	Offer	Shipping
TablePro	79	5 for 4	£5 per table
Furnitr	89	10 for 9	Free

Example Test Question: Work out which supplier offers the best value for money (including shipping costs).

1. First work out how many we need to pay for:

TablePro	Furnitr
$\frac{4}{5}$ of 115 $= 92$	$\frac{9}{10}$ of 115 $= 103.5$
So we pay for 92 with table pro	We pay for 104 with Furnitr

2. Work out the cost for the tables.

TablePro	Furnitr
$79 \times 92 = £7,268$	$104 \times 89 = £9,256$

3. Add the shipping

TablePro	Furnitr
$5 \times 115 = £575$	**Free Delivery**
$£7,268 + £575 = £7,843$	
Total Cost = £7,843	**Total Cost** = £9,256

From this we can see that **TablePro** is the cheaper option to order the 115 tables from.

11.4 I can work out the best price when considering discounts and offers – TEST questions

a) Work out how much cheaper it is to buy 14 packets of felt-tips from SuperStationer in comparison to BargainPens.

	Cost per pack (£)	Offer	Delivery
SuperStationer	1.99	Buy one get one free	£4.95
BargainPens	1.89	Three for two	Free

b) A school prints out 230 paper registers each day for 195 days a year. Each register costs £0.02. An annual subscription to a digital register website costs £73.95 each year. Work out which option, paper or online register copies, is cheaper and by how much.

c) A head teacher has to decide whether to employ a supply teacher at a cost of £32 per hour for 900 hours a year plus £450 finder's fee, or a full-time member of staff for 950 hours at a cost of £30 per hour. Which option is the most cost effective?

d) Thornbramble Elementary needs to purchase 14,000 workbooks for the next academic year. Using the schools purchasing system the administrator has produced the following table.

Supplier	Cost per 1000 (£)	Offer	Delivery
A	890	10% off	Free
B	840	Five for four	£3.99 per 1000
C	815	No offer.	Free

Which is the most cost effective option?

e) Cutting the school field each year costs £72 for each day it is cut by an external company for the first ten times, then £65 for each day after. The school requires the grass cutting 26 times a year. Alternatively, the school can buy a lawnmower at a cost of £2,199 and claim back 20% for VAT. Which is the most expensive option for the school over the period of 1 year?

f) A school canteen purchases 4000kg of potatoes per year. They can choose between two suppliers which are displayed in the table below.

Shop	Weight of bag	Cost (£)	Offer
PotatoChief	25kg	7.99	None.
FresherPotaoes	5kg	£1.95	Buy two, get one free.

Which is the cheapest supplier?

g) A printer costs £1,485 to buy, with each toner cartridge costing £56.00, on a buy two get one free offer. Each toner prints 10,000 sheets. Alternatively, the school can hire a printer at a cost of £0.01 per sheet printed. In one school year, the school prints 250,000 sheets. Which option is the cheapest for one year, purchase or hire?

h) Fleetwood High bulk buys school jumpers each year.

| | Size Cost (£) | | | |
Shop	Small	Medium	Large	Offer
UniFormPro	7.99	7.99	7.99	10% off small jumpers
ClothingLtd	7.99	8.99	9.99	15% of total price

For the next school year, the school needs to purchase:

200 small,

650 medium,

and 400 large

Which shop, UniFormPro or ClothingLtd would be the cheapest option?

12. Full Practice Test

Visit **QTS Maths Tutor** to take our full free practice test in exam conditions.

These tests have been designed to mimic the real numeracy skills test as much as possible.

Just visit https://www.qtsmathstutor.co.uk/ and click **Free Practice Test**.

Looking for Literacy Skills Practise?

Visit: http://literacyskillstest.co.uk/ for practice tests, tutors and much more.

Take our **Free Literacy Skills Test** Now!

QTS MATHS TUTOR
WWW.QTSMATHSTUTOR.CO.UK

FREE ONLINE NUMERACY SKILLS TEST
EXPERT 1 TO 1 TUITION WITH OUR QTS SPECIALISTS

--- **WHAT QTS MATHS TUTOR HAS TO OFFER** ---

**21 Numeracy
Skills Tests**

**12 Topic
Revision Tests**

**Over 120
Video Solutions**

**Regularly Updated
Questions**

**Expert 1 to 1
Tuition Service**

**Written Solutions
to every question**

Visit **www.qtsmathstutor.co.uk** to take a <u>Free Full Practice Test today.</u>

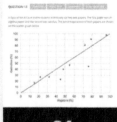

21
NUMERACY SKILLS TESTS

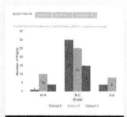

12
TOPIC REVISION TESTS

650+
MODEL SOLUTIONS

QTS LITERACY TUTOR
WWW.LITERACYSKILLSTEST.CO.UK

 Based on hundreds of reviews on ★ Trustpilot

FREE ONLINE LITERACY SKILLS TEST
EXPERT 1 TO 1 TUITION WITH OUR QTS SPECIALISTS

— WHAT QTS LITERACY TUTOR HAS TO OFFER —

Spelling Practice

Punctuation Questions

Grammar Section

Comprehension Resources

Practice Tests

Expert Tutors

Correct Format

New Question Formats

Visit www.literacyskillstest.co.uk to take a Free Full Practice Test today.

10
LITERACY SKILLS TESTS

97%
LEARNER PASS RATE

490
TEST QUESTIONS

Answers

1.1   I can multiply numbers from 1 to 12 - SKILLS answers

a) 108   b) 24   c) 15   d) 66   e) 60   f) 33   g) 22   h) 176

i) 240   j) 280   k) 126   l) 396   m) 144   n) 396   o) 160   p) 330

q) 576   r) 200   s) 20   t) 1600   u) 2772   v) 3150   w) 1701   x) 1452

y) 640   z) 420

1.2   I can multiply numbers from 1 to 12 - TEST answers

a) 188   b) 144   c) 30   d) 84   e) 66   f) 32   g) 35   h) 27

i) 30   j) 24   k) 66   l) 72   m) 24   n) 21   o) 112   p) 86

q) 56   r) 148   s) 43   t) 68   u) 94   v) 50   w) 60   x) 32

y) 164   z) 96

1.4   I can use the grid multiplication method - SKILLS answers

a) 168   b) 3840   c) 5680   d) 1144   e) 675

f) 4710   g) 57300   h) 26474   i) 457028   j) 696192

k) 45367   l) 413406   m) 1312443   n) 16106100   o) 42482556

p) 488030   q) 6014694   r) 72625896   s) 359599149   t) 5653304196

u) 4761105   v) 11165735   w) 241500604   x) 1059859119   y) 64629948992

z) 80779853376

1.5   I can use the grid multiplication method - TEST answers

a) 28.88   b) 11.04   c) 3660   d) 132   e) 4.2   f) 530

g) 143   h) 125   i) 31.50   j) 1015   k) 3325   l) 193.44

m) 122   n) 2500   o) 99   p) 107.64   q) 628   r) 274

s) 134   t) 4.2   u) 2945   v) 800   w) 10000   x) 1095

y) 5390   z) 2765

1.7   I can multiply by fractions – SKILLS answers

a) $\frac{1}{6}$ b) $\frac{1}{24}$ c) $\frac{1}{18}$ d) $\frac{4}{15}$ e) $\frac{1}{12}$ f) $\frac{2}{7}$ g) $\frac{7}{27}$ h) $\frac{16}{45}$

i) $\frac{36}{49}$ j) $\frac{1}{9}$ k) 15   l) 25   m) 33   n) 25   o) 25   p) 44

q) 22   r) 15   s) 50   t) 7   u) 32   v) 100   w) 66   x) 30

y) 49   z) 42

1.8   I can multiply by fractions – TEST answers

a) 315   b) $\frac{3}{14}$ c) 100   d) $\frac{1}{8}$ e) $\frac{3}{25}$ f) 50   g) 200   h) 12

i) 25   j) $\frac{7}{16}$ k) 70   l) $\frac{2}{5}$ m) $\frac{3}{56}$ n) $\frac{4}{15}$ o) 5   p) 45

q) $\frac{7}{30}$ r) $\frac{5}{7}$ s) $\frac{7}{16}$ t) 20   u) $\frac{4}{9}$ v) $\frac{32}{45}$ w) 40   x) 35

y) 30   z) 225

1.10   I can multiply by decimals – SKILLS answers

a) 0.1   b) 269.7   c) 76.8   d) 2.62   e) 0.25

f) 1   g) 0.0124   h) 0.375   i) 26.24   j) 8.25

k) 39   l) 56.07   m) 31.32   n) 0.9116   o) 36.3268

p) 0.1892   q) 5.4498   r) 4.4368   s) 0.2236   t) 123.662

u) 13.6102   v) 0.004417   w) 0.07326   x) 2.961992   y) 501.800775

z) 22.76912

1.11 I can multiply by decimals – TEST answers

a) 33 b) 50 c) 70 d) 73.15 e) 35.70 f)13.60

g) 4.30 h) 22.80 i) 9.50 j) 51 k) 29 l) 12.20

m) 18.40 n) 225 o) 28.70 p) 25 q) 19.90 r) 40.20

s) 22.05 t) 39 u) 27.25 v) 31.50 w) 65.20 x) 10

y) 11.75 z) 9.50

2.1 I can perform division using the standard method – SKILLS answers

a) 1.25 b) 1.13 c) 1.5 d) 4 e) 1 f) 3.47

g) 11.25 h) 15.83 i) 9.25 j) 1.67 k) 11.5 l) 30.8

m) 13 n) 24.35 o) 173 p) 112.2 q) 124.5 r) 175.67

s) 686.13 t) 58.7 u) 1421.29 v) 27.58 w) 1073.25 x) 194.23

y) 975.3 z) 118.30

2.2 I can perform division using the standard method – TEST answers

a) 48.5 b) 30.5 c) 27.5 d) 34.5 e) 24 f) 2 g) 7.5 h) 2

i) 9 j) 8.5 k) 51.5 l) 66 m) 50.5 n) 7 o) 7.5 p) 7

q) 6 r) 3.5 s) 3.50 t) 7 u) 5 v) 9 w) 2.5 x) 6

y) 1 z) 1.5

2.4   I can solve decimal division questions – SKILLS answers

a) 0.3   b) 0.87   c) 2.8   d) 11   e) 8   f) 5

g) 400   h) 10.5   i) 3300   j) 125   k) 5.5   l) 1000

m) 7070   n) 20000   o) 1   p) 350   q) 40   r) 1.43

s) 1000   t) 195   u) 1732.5   v) 2.78   w) 2311000   x) 12345.6

y) 10483.33   z) 3.14

2.5   I can solve decimal division questions – TEST answers

a) 24300   b) 41235   c) 8230   d) 72900   e) 2743500   f) 52800

g) 12660   h) 45215   i) 2965   j) 20560   k) 11870   l) 45670

m) 24700   n) 3620   o) 1320   p) 70900   q) 302000   r) 9870

s) 13255   t) 1731900   u) 155000   v) 1650   w) 1368300   x) 19405

y) 96700   z) 41300

3.1   I can simplify fractions – SKILLS answers

a) $\frac{1}{2}$ b) $\frac{1}{9}$ c) $\frac{1}{4}$ d) $\frac{1}{10}$ e) $\frac{1}{6}$ f) $\frac{1}{7}$ g) $\frac{1}{3}$ h) $\frac{1}{5}$

i) $\frac{1}{11}$ j) $\frac{1}{8}$ k) $\frac{1}{12}$ l) $\frac{2}{3}$ m) $\frac{2}{7}$ n) $\frac{2}{5}$ o) $\frac{2}{9}$ p) $\frac{2}{11}$

q) $\frac{3}{5}$ r) $\frac{5}{7}$ s) $\frac{6}{7}$ t) $\frac{11}{15}$ u) $\frac{3}{7}$ v) $\frac{3}{13}$ w) $\frac{2}{7}$ x) $\frac{24}{25}$

y) $\frac{19}{20}$ z) $\frac{29}{30}$

3.2   I can simplify fractions – TEST answers

a) $\frac{1}{4}$ b) $\frac{9}{10}$ c) $\frac{5}{7}$ d) $\frac{2}{3}$ e) $\frac{9}{10}$ f) $\frac{3}{4}$ g) $\frac{4}{7}$ h) $\frac{1}{15}$

i) $\frac{1}{15}$ j) $\frac{5}{6}$ k) $\frac{1}{3}$ l) $\frac{8}{9}$ m) $\frac{1}{20}$ n) $\frac{5}{6}$ o) $\frac{2}{3}$ p) $\frac{14}{15}$

q) $\frac{3}{4}$ r) $\frac{2}{9}$ s) $\frac{1}{20}$ t) $\frac{7}{8}$ u) $\frac{2}{5}$ v) $\frac{3}{4}$ w) $\frac{1}{9}$ x) $\frac{2}{9}$

y) $\frac{2}{7}$ z) $\frac{1}{3}$

a) $\dfrac{1}{2}$ = 0.5 = 50%   b) $\dfrac{1}{3}$ = 0.333 = 33.33%

c) $\dfrac{1}{4}$ = 0.25 = 25%   d) $\dfrac{1}{5}$ = 0.2 = 20%

e) $\dfrac{1}{6}$ = 0.167 = 16.67%   f) $\dfrac{1}{7}$ = 0.1429 = 14.29%

g) $\dfrac{1}{8}$ = 0.125 = 12.50%   h) $\dfrac{1}{10}$ = 0.1 = 10%

i) $\dfrac{1}{25}$ = 0.04 = 4%   j) $\dfrac{1}{50}$ = 0.02 = 2%

k) $\dfrac{3}{5}$ = 0.6 = 60%   l) $\dfrac{4}{10}$ = 0.4 = 40%

m) $\dfrac{3}{25}$ = 0.12 = 12%   n) $\dfrac{16}{50}$ = 0.32 = 32%

o) $\dfrac{3}{4}$ = 0.75 = 75%   p) $\dfrac{2}{3}$ = 0.6667 = 66.67%

q) $\dfrac{68}{20}$ = 0.34 = 34%   r) $\dfrac{24}{120}$ = 0.2 = 20%

s) $\dfrac{6}{40}$ = 0.15 = 15%   t) $\dfrac{9}{12}$ = 0.75 = 75%

u) $\dfrac{3}{12}$ = 0.25 = 25%   v) $\dfrac{4}{5}$ = 0.8 = 80%

w) $\dfrac{24}{25}$ = 0.96 = 96%   x) $\dfrac{1}{15}$ = 0.0667 = 6.67%

y) $\dfrac{5}{8}$ = 0.625 = 62.5%   z) $\dfrac{4}{11}$ = 0.3636 = 36.36%

.5   I can convert between fractions, decimals and percentages – TEST answers

a) 0.1   b) 90%   c) 0.83   d) 0.33   e) 0.25   f) 87.5%

g) 0.17   h) 0.2   i) 12.5%   j) 10%   k) 0.2   l) 0.5

m) 0.2   n) 25%   o) 0.25   p) 80%   q) 0.1   r) 0.83

s) 16.67%   t) 16.67%   u) 12.5%   v) 0.17   w) 87.5%   x) 10%

y) 0.1   z) 90%

.7   I can calculate a proportion of an amount - SKILLS answers

a) 78.75   b) 52   c) 16.25   d) 84.75   e) 260   f) 260

g) 333   h) 195   i) 49.5   j) 201.25   k) 216.75   l) 273

m) 364.5   n) 7.5   o) 238   p) 270   q) 171   r) 382

s) 96.5   t) 782   u) 476   v) 294   w) 156   x) 23.75

y) 6.5   z) 372

.8   I can calculate a proportion of an amount – TEST answers

a) 16   b) 135   c) £315   d) 45   e) £140   f) £420

g) 70   h) £25   i) 5   j) £20   k) £120   l) £385

m) 55   n) 7   o) £75   p) £168   q) £90   r) 495

s) £15   t) 3   u) 50   v) £300   w) 360   x) 55

y) 5   z) 100

.1   I can calculate percentage increase and decrease – TEST answers

a) £1.50   b) 185   c) 83   d) 57   e) 85.5 m   f) 36

g) 11.25   h) 44   i) 162   j) 152   k) 26.55   l) £26.40

m) 136   n) 8.25   o) £61.05   p) £123.25   q) 95   r) 44

s) 81   t) 1615   u) 170   v) 180.5   w) 74.25   x) 87

y) 68   z) 66

.2   I can convert between currencies and distances – TEST answers

a) £240   b) ¥884   c) ¥726   d) €1296   e) ¥1908

f) £120 g) £380 h) ¥836 i) €714 j) €572

k) €1200 l) ¥784 m) $1368 n) $420 o) 975 miles

p) 590 miles q) 690 miles r) 712 km s) 235 miles t) 165 miles

u) 40 km v) 555 miles w) 160 km x) 410 miles y) 664 km

z) 392 km

5.4   I can simplify and divide into ratios – TEST answers

a) 24 b) 150 c) 4 d) 96 e) 20 f) 9 g) 9 h) 14

i) 24 j) 72 k) 45 l) 16 m) 8 n) 2 o) 9 p) 36

q) 16 r) 15 s) 24 t) 130 u) 22 v) 14 w) 18 x) 18

y) 27 z) 28

6.1   I can solve problems that involve time – TEST answers

a) 2 pm b) 2hr 35m c) 12:12 pm d) 36hr 40m e) 3.15 pm

f) 3.45 pm g) 24hr 40m h) 22hrs i) 38hr 50m j) 19hrs

k) 4.40 pm l) 11.11 am m) 7.05 pm n) 10hr 15m o) 1.35 pm

p) 4.25 pm q) 6.10 pm r) 7.15 pm s) 1m 30s t) 1.45 pm

u) 7hr 5m v) 7hr 30m w) 1.50 pm x) 9.30 pm y) 4hr 20m

z) 2.35 pm

7.1   I can calculate perimeter, area and volume – TEST answers

a) 150 cm
b) 5600000 cm^3
c) 9600 cm^2
d) 7500 cm^2

e) 3200 m^2
f) 3840000 cm^3
g) 2100000 cm^3
h) 18850 m^2

i) 720000 cm^3
j) 580 m
k) 210 mm
l) 7600 cm^2

m) 360000 cm^3
n) 130000 cm^3
o) 1800 cm^2
p) 12000 m^2

q) 4800000 cm^3
r) 5950 m^2
s) 2250 cm^2
t) 370 cm

u) 7350 cm^2
v) 280000 cm^3
w) 3000 cm^2
x) 150 m^3

y) 200 m
z) 13775 m^2

8.2   I can perform multiplication using a calculator – TEST answers

a) £2,782.50
b) £4.14
c) £838.50
d) £62.30

e) £58.84
f) £1,891.93
g) £2,570

8.4   I can perform division using a calculator – TEST answers

a) £2.95
b) 7
c) £115.00
d) Beatrice

e) 5
f) £6.00
g) 21.2m^2

8.6   I can perform compound conversions - TEST answers

a) £4.20 per gallon
b) 0.24 km/m
c) 29.96 mph
d) 4.57 mm/h

e) €2.45
f) 19.3 g/cm^3
g) £5.63 per gallon

9.2 I can work out the mean, median, mode and range – SKILLS answers

	Mean	Median	Mode	Range		Mean	Median	Mode	Range
a)	3	4	4	3	i)	3.18	3.2	NA	2.1
b)	5.4	6	6	3	j)	0.4	0.4	NA	0.8
c)	4.33	4.5	7	6	k)	0.38	0.3	NA	0.9
d)	23.5	11	NA	79	l)	0.64	0.7	0.5	0.3
e)	37.67	21	NA	92	m)	1.5	1.5	1.5	2
f)	24.25	24.5	NA	44	n)	13.68	15	15	20
g)	28.29	29	NA	42	o)	3.30	3	4	4
h)	0.57	1	1	1	p)	2.96	3	5	4

9.3 I can work out the mean, median, mode and range – TEST answers

a)
| i) FALSE | ii) TRUE | iii) FALSE | iv) TRUE | v) TRUE | vi) FALSE |
| vii) TRUE | viii) FALSE | ix) FALSE | x) TRUE | xi) TRUE | xii) TRUE |

b)
| i) FALSE | ii) TRUE | iii) FALSE | iv) FALSE | v) TRUE | vi) FALSE |
| vii) FALSE | viii) FALSE | ix) TRUE | x) TRUE | xi) FALSE | xii) TRUE |

c)
| i) TRUE | ii) TRUE | iii) FALSE | iv) TRUE | v) TRUE | vi) FALSE |
| vii) FALSE | viii) FALSE | ix) TRUE | x) FALSE | xi) TRUE | xii) TRUE |

9.5   I can work out possible values using a summary table – TEST answers

a)
| i)TRUE | ii)TRUE | iii)FALSE | iv) TRUE | v)TRUE | vi)TRUE |
| vii)FALSE | viii)TRUE | ix)TRUE | x) FALSE | xi)TRUE | xii)FALSE |

b)
| i)FALSE | ii)FALSE | iii)TRUE | iv)FALSE | v)TRUE | vi)TRUE |
| vii)FALSE | viii)TRUE | ix)TRUE | x)FALSE | xi)TRUE | xii)TRUE |

c)
| i)FALSE | ii)TRUE | iii)TRUE | iv)FALSE | v)FALSE | vi)TRUE |
| vii)TRUE | viii)FALSE | ix)TRUE | x)FALSE | xi)TRUE | xii)TRUE |

10.2   I can make inferences using a box plot – TEST answers

a)
| i)TRUE | ii)TRUE | iii)TRUE | iv)FALSE | v)TRUE | vi)TRUE |
| vii)FALSE | viii)TRUE | ix)FALSE | x)TRUE | xi)TRUE | xii)TRUE |

b)
| i)TRUE | ii)TRUE | iii)FALSE | iv)FALSE | v)TRUE | vi)FALSE |
| vii)TRUE | viii)FALSE | ix)TRUE | x)FALSE | xi)TRUE | xii)TRUE |

c)
| i)FALSE | ii)FALSE | iii)TRUE | iv)TRUE | v)FALSE | vi)TRUE |
| vii)TRUE | viii)TRUE | ix)TRUE | x)FALSE | xi)FALSE | xii)FALSE |

10.4   I can make inferences using a scatter graph – TEST answers

a)
| i)TRUE | ii)FALSE | iii)TRUE | iv)FALSE | v)TRUE | vi)TRUE |
| vii)FALSE | viii)FALSE | ix)FALSE | x)TRUE | xi)FALSE | xii)TRUE |

b)
| i)TRUE | ii)FALSE | iii)TRUE | iv)FALSE | v)TRUE | vi)TRUE |
| vii)FALSE | viii)FALSE | ix)FALSE | x)TRUE | xi)FALSE | xii)FALSE |

c)
| i)FALSE | ii)FALSE | iii)FALSE | iv)FALSE | v)TRUE | vi)TRUE |
| vii)TRUE | viii)FALSE | ix)FALSE | x)TRUE | xi)TRUE | xii)TRUE |

10.6   I can make inferences using a line graph – TEST answers

a)
| i)TRUE | ii)TRUE | iii)FALSE | iv)TRUE | v)FALSE | vi)FALSE |
| vii)TRUE | viii)TRUE | ix)TRUE | x)FALSE | xi)TRUE | xii)FALSE |

b)
| i)FALSE | ii)TRUE | iii)TRUE | iv)FALSE | v)FALSE | vi)FALSE |
| vii)FALSE | viii)FALSE | ix)TRUE | x)FALSE | xi)FALSE | xii)TRUE |

c)
| i)TRUE | ii)FALSE | iii)TRUE | iv)TRUE | v)TRUE | vi)FALSE |
| vii)TRUE | viii)TRUE | ix)FALSE | x)TRUE | xi)FALSE | xii)FALSE |

10.8 I can make inferences using a bar chart – TEST answers

a)

i)TRUE	ii)TRUE	iii)FALSE	iv)TRUE	v)FALSE	vi)FALSE
vii)FALSE	viii)FALSE	ix)TRUE	x)FALSE	xi)FALSE	xii)FALSE

b)

i)TRUE	ii)FALSE	iii)FALSE	iv)TRUE	v)FALSE	vi)FALSE
vii)FALSE	viii)TRUE	ix)TRUE	x)FALSE	xi)TRUE	xii)FALSE

c)

i)TRUE	ii)FALSE	iii)TRUE	iv)TRUE	v)FALSE	vi)TRUE
vii)FALSE	viii)TRUE	ix)FALSE	x)FALSE	xi)TRUE	xii)FALSE

10.10 I can make inferences using a cumulative frequency graph – TEST answers

a)

i)TRUE	ii)FALSE	iii)FALSE	iv)FALSE	v)FALSE	vi)TRUE
vii)TRUE	viii)FALSE	ix)TRUE			

b)

i)TRUE	ii)TRUE	iii)TRUE	iv)FALSE	v)FALSE	vi)TRUE
vii)TRUE	viii)FALSE	ix)TRUE			

10.12 I can make inferences using a pie chart – TEST answers

a)

i)TRUE	ii)FALSE	iii)FALSE	iv)TRUE	v)FALSE	vi)TRUE
vii)TRUE	viii)FALSE	ix)TRUE	x)FALSE	xi)FALSE	xii)FALSE

b)

i)FALSE	ii)FALSE	iii)TRUE	iv)TRUE	v)TRUE	vi)TRUE
vii)TRUE	viii)TRUE	ix)TRUE	x)FALSE	xi)FALSE	xii)FALSE

c)

i)FALSE	ii)FALSE	iii)FALSE	iv)FALSE	v)FALSE	vi)TRUE
vii)TRUE	viii)FALSE	ix)TRUE	x)FALSE	xi)TRUE	xii)TRUE

10.14 I can make inferences using a two-way table – TEST answers

a)

i)TRUE	ii)FALSE	iii)FALSE	iv)TRUE	v)FALSE	vi)FALSE
vii)FALSE	viii)FALSE	ix)TRUE	x)TRUE	xi)FALSE	xii)TRUE

b)

i)TRUE	ii)TRUE	iii)TRUE	iv)FALSE	v)TRUE	vi)FALSE
vii)FALSE	viii)TRUE	ix)FALSE	x)FALSE	xi)TRUE	xii)TRUE

c)

i)FALSE	ii)TRUE	iii)TRUE	iv)TRUE	v)TRUE	vi)TRUE
vii)TRUE	viii)FALSE	ix)FALSE	x)FALSE	xi)FALSE	xii)TRUE

11.2 I can work with formulas and weighting – TEST answers

a) Charlie – 63.4

b) 95°C

c) 180.5cm^2 (195.5 – 15)

d) 1.97 siblings

e) Tanya – 77.5

f) 267.947 cm^3

g) 45.8

h) £10,200

11.4 I can work out the best price when considering discounts and offers - TEST answers

a) Super at £18.88

b) E-register saves £823.05

c) Fulltime at £28,500 supply (29,250)

d) Supplier B £9463.86

e) Purchase mower at £1759.20

f) FresherPotatoes £1041.3

g) Purchase £2437

h) ClothingLtd £9721.88

Printed in Great Britain
by Amazon